Getting Over

Depression

My Testimony of how I wanted to give up, but God wouldn't let me because He had a greater plan for my life!

Mark Buckley

"For I know the thoughts that I think toward you, says the LORD, thoughts of peace and not of evil, to give you a future and a hope."

— Jeremiah 29:11

Have You Ever Experienced Depression?

- Do You Dislike Who you are?
- Have problems with anger?
- Feel as if you don't fit in?
- Do you think life is more of a burden than a blessing?

Depression is real and affects more than one out of five people, and it is Satan's greatest weapon.

Getting Over Depression is an account of my life experiences and the feelings that accompanied them. I think you'll discover that, although my situation might be different from yours, you may have experienced similar emotions and thoughts. Emotions and thoughts that might be destroying your very life and that of your family.

During my depression, I thought I was the only one who felt or thought the way I did and was unable to share those feelings with others. Be assured you're not the only one, as you'll soon discover as I show you how I viewed life and the consequences of that view.

I will share my journey of recovery from a man who continually wanted to end his life to a man who can't wait to see what wonderful things tomorrow will bring. I can look at the past that used to haunt me, but it now brings me peace. I now see that everything really does happen for a reason and how our lives affect those around us.

If you're reading this book, you're reading it for a reason — a reason you may not be aware of yet. Something you'll read here will help you or someone you know or love; I pray you receive the gift of peace.

— **Mark Buckley**

gettingoverdepression.org

Contents

Page Left Blank Intentionally

Introduction

This book shows the way I used to look at life when I was suffering from depression and the way God has shown me to see life now. I can now look at the past that used to haunt me in a way that brings me peace. I have gone through a lot in my life, but who hasn't? I have gone through extensive treatment for depression and have been diagnosed with bi-polar, chemical imbalance, manic depression, and seizure disorder, along with being treated for repeated suicide attempts. I was nineteen when I began treatment for my depression and received treatment until I was forty-six years old. Treatment included more medication than I can remember, therapy, hospitalization, and Electro-shock therapy. I had a life I couldn't adjust to and just wanted it to end. My life seemed to have no meaning or purpose, and that's a terrible place to be.

When God finally got my attention and knocked some sense into me, I heard a saying that I will never forget, "God never wastes a hurt." As I look back on my life, I can see how God helped me through all the tough times that I put myself and others through. I can see that everything happens for a reason, and I can see how our lives affect others and how they are all part of God's plan. If you are reading this book, you are reading it for a reason. There may be something that you'll read that will help you or someone you know or love. There could be something in your life that is troubling you, and you are looking for an answer, and part of the answer may just happen to be in this book. All you need to do is ask yourself, "What does God want me to receive from reading this book?"

When I started asking myself why God had put me in a particular place at that time and what I was supposed to learn, I started seeing the answers. People began to give me books that entered my life. I was going to church and listening to sermons, and each one had a message just for me; they were all leading me in a specific direction. I discovered that the answers I was looking for were all around me; all I had to do was open my heart to receive them. As I received the answers to my problems, I started sharing my experiences with others and discovered what it was that God wanted me to do. God has revealed to me that I am supposed to try to help others with their depression. I feel God is now able to use me because I finally stopped trying to run my life for me and gave my life to Him.

I ask that you read this book with an open mind and heart. On these pages, there is a special gift just for you, and all you need to do is recognize it. Let God begin to work in your life; He loves us all so much and wants to help us. When you discover what it is you are supposed to get from this book, it will help to make your life easier and give you some of the answers you may have been looking for. That's the time to get down on your knees and thank Him. Every gift we receive is from God, and when we come to realize that we can attain a real sense of peace in our lives.

— **Mark Buckley**

Chapter One — A Beautiful Day

I woke up to the sun shining on my face through the window. It was another beautiful morning in Southern California. I went out on the balcony and looked out to see neighboring homes with well-manicured yards, each accented with a variety of shrubs and plants. I looked down to see my own yard and the walkway, which had roses of different colors bordering it. The sun glistened off the dew so brightly I had to squint to see. I went inside to get ready for my journey. I shaved, brushed my teeth, took a shower, and selected the clothes I would wear for that day. I went downstairs to the kitchen to grab something to eat before I left. I took a bagel from the refrigerator and placed it in the toaster to brown.

While I was waiting, I went to the side door to admire my handy work in the yard from the week before. I trimmed back the bushes that had become overgrown and cleaned up the beds of unwanted weeds. After my bagel popped up from the toaster, I spread a generous portion of my favorite cream cheese over the top and proceeded to go to the back door. I went out through the sliding glass door to my deck and went past my hot tub to the railing. The hill in my backyard was in full bloom of bright red flowers, and the trees on the top made the perfect fence, giving me seclusion from the outside world. Today is going to be a very special day for me. I've been planning a trip to my favorite place, the Cove at La Jolla. The Cove at La Jolla is where I fell in love with California about sixteen months earlier, and it was the reason I decided California was going to be my new home.

Since I moved to California, I have taken several trips to that special place, but this morning, my trip to La Jolla was going to be different as I embarked alone. I decided to take the scenic route on the coast highway. With my windows down and my sunroof opened, I enjoyed the sun and the wind as it filled my car. I enjoyed going through the small towns, looking at the shops and people walking on the sidewalks. I reached one of my favorite spots where the road winds up on top of a mountain, and you can look down and see the coastline for miles on a clear day. I watched in amazement while enjoying the fragrance of the salt air. I passed several white sandy beaches that had dozens of surfers heading out to the cool water to catch a wave before work. There wasn't a cloud in the sky, and the bright blue reflected off the water like a mirror. I chose the perfect day to end my life.

Yes, that's what I'd been planning for the last six days. I took a couple of items: a bottle of water and a container filled with a powerful anti-depressant. I was truly excited and relieved about my final trip to the cove. In my own way, I said good-bye to my wife, son, and daughter. None of them knew of my final trip. It was an early Monday morning, so the cove wasn't very busy, and I was able to find a good spot close to the water. It was a smooth, flat rock with no one nearby; it was as if I had the whole beach to myself. I sat down on the rock and placed my bottle of water next to me. I sat for a while, enjoying the great view I had, listening to the waves and the birds flying over the water. I thought to myself, today will be the day all the hurting ends, and peace will come over me. I wasn't nervous, only relieved that this terrible thing I called life was about to end.

I lived in Ohio most of my life; a couple of years earlier, I visited California. I was at the cove in La Jolla, and I felt as if something was calling me. I just stood there for over an hour looking out over the ocean, and I finally figured out why I was so depressed. I wasn't living in California! Boy, that was easy. Without preparation and just on an impulse, I moved six months later. Well, for some reason, things still weren't going right, and less than a year later, I found myself without a job and on the verge of losing my home.

One day, I decided it would be best for everyone if I was no longer here. I remember waking up in the morning and despising the reflection I saw in the mirror to the point I would talk to myself and tell myself what a terrible person I was. I didn't even try to defend myself. I took a bottle of pills and headed back to the beach, where I fell in love with California. This is now my sixth suicide attempt. The first one, I hired someone to kill me (the person went to the wrong place), another was by electrocution (a phone call stopped me at the last moment), I was going to shoot myself (someone stopped me and found the gun), and a couple of overdoses (not quite enough I guess).

How did I get to this point where something as precious as life became a burden instead of a blessing? How could I sit and see something so beautiful and be glad that I'll never see it again? What could have happened to me that I thought so little of living when I had so much to live for? Why did I spend more time thinking about how to end my life instead of living it?

Getting Over Depression

Have you ever said, "I wish I was never born?" It's amazing how we can feel so bad at one moment that we are able to disregard an entire lifetime of blessings.

At 19, I was diagnosed as having a seizure disorder, and through the years that followed, the diagnoses included bipolar disorder, chemical imbalance, and manic depressive. I was treated with just about every known anti-depressant imaginable, hospitalized several times for depression, and, as a last resort, given electroshock therapy.

So why was I so depressed? The doctors had all kinds of reasons, from emotional to physical, but I believe it was my focus. Life is like a camera; whatever you focus on is what develops. My focus was on myself. I was constantly looking at things with me as the central focus, no matter what it was. If my family wanted to do something, it depended on how I felt. If there was something I wanted, I bought it. No matter what was going on, I looked at how it affected me. I was always searching for peace and happiness, and believe me, I went to every store imaginable and didn't find it. During my life, I have had over forty jobs, lived in over thirty places, and couldn't even count the number of cars and toys I bought, looking for peace of mind. I would have done just about anything to change the state of mind I was in. I look back now and wonder what I was leaving behind for others besides the insurance money.

In the forty-six years of my existence, what had I contributed? Was there anyone that would say that because of me, they were a better person? What legacy was I leaving for my children? "When the going gets tough, go!" was that my epitaph? I was so focused on myself that I wasn't able to do anything for anyone else, so I came into the world alone and left the same way. Instead of bringing joy, I brought pain and heartache to the people who loved me. What a waste. So why am I still here? I asked that question more times than I can remember. I discovered if you're still here, God's not done with you.

I sat on that rock, looking over the beautiful ocean. As I sat there, I listened to the sounds the waves made crashing over the rocks. I took my candy box of pills out of my pocket and opened it. I looked over the ocean, and for the first time in my life, I decided to talk to God. I said, "God, I understand that I don't deserve to be in heaven for what I'm about to do, and I understand why you wouldn't want me there, but I don't believe I belong in hell either. I've been an okay person; there isn't anyone who could say I did anything terrible to them. I was never unfaithful to my wife, and I treated my parents with respect. I loved my children and have tried to take care of their needs. How about we just end it here? Let me just go to sleep and never wake up, and it will be as if I was never here. It would have been better if I wasn't here anyway. What do you say? Is it a deal?"

I waited a moment, almost expecting a response. "Do you believe that the first time I decided to talk to God, I told him He messed up? I was saying, you made a mistake; you made me. You did okay with the earth, ocean, mountains, and the universe in general, but when you made me, you must have been having a bad day."

When it was obvious God wasn't going to answer me, I took the pills, then sat there and asked God for another favor, "Please, God, I don't mind dying; just don't let it hurt." I had ignored God all my life, and now I started asking for favors. I sat there wondering what was going to happen, wondering if the medication was ever going to take effect, and then suddenly, everything started to spin. I felt a wrenching in my stomach, and it took everything for me not to throw-up. I started to feel this horrible pain in my head. I yelled, "I asked for no pain," as if I had really made a deal. I started to shake uncontrollably, and it felt as if my heart was going to explode. The beating was so heavy I could feel it in my hands and feet. The pressure in my head was so severe I thought my eyes were going to pop out of their sockets. I pleaded to God, "Please don't let it hurt anymore; make it stop." By now, everything on the beach appeared to be moving, and then it became dark. It appeared my prayer was answered, and the answer was no.

How many times do you pray and feel your prayer wasn't answered because God didn't answer in the way and timing you wanted? We forget that '*no*' is an answer. Remember when you were a child, how many of your requests were answered with a no because your parents felt that what you were asking was not good for you, or how many times as a parent did you tell your child no instead of yes because you felt you knew better and wanted to keep your child safe. Our Father is the perfect parent and knows what is best for us and sees everything and how it can affect us in the future.

"If you then, being evil, know how to give good gifts to your children, how much more will your Father who is in heaven give good things to those who ask Him!"

— **Matthew 7:11**

I took enough medication to kill at least three people. I took the pills around nine thirty that morning and went into a coma. I must have been sitting on that rock looking up into the sky until six o'clock that evening. Someone walking on the beach saw me fall off the rock into the sand and called 911. My face was burnt and peeling from the sun. My arms, with my palms pointing up, were laying on my legs as if I were presenting a gift to someone. You could see the outline of my arms on my sunburned legs, and my arms were burned. All day long, I must have followed the sun because, as burned as my face was, the top of my head was barely red at all.

I was taken to the hospital, where my family was called in and told they were not sure if I was going to make it. If I did survive, I might have severe liver problems, and they were not sure how much brain damage was caused. I was in a coma for a couple of days and awoke with no side effects. Though family and friends wondered about how much brain damage I had before the overdose.

When I woke up, my mind wasn't clear, and I was confused about what had happened. Then it came to me, and I couldn't believe I was still alive. Why would God do this to me? There are people all over the earth dying who would give anything to stay alive, and all I wanted was to die. Everything in my life has been about me. I made as if I thought about my family when I decided to commit suicide, but it was the easy way out for me. I looked at my family and saw my daughter, whose eyes were swollen from crying. I asked her for a hug and kiss. As she approached the bed, I saw her back up as if she wasn't going to come to me, and then she quickly hugged me, gave me a peck on the cheek, and stepped away.

I assumed then that it was that she was unsure and was sorting out an array of feelings she was going through. She confided in me later that after baking in the sun for a day and not bathing for a couple of days or brushing my teeth, I stunk. I was still covered with sand and had cuts from falling over onto rocks. It was not one of my cuddlier and kissable moments. I looked up at my sister, waiting to hear some loving sentiment that would ease my pain.

She looked down at me and said, "You owe your wife an apology. How can you be so insensitive? Do you have any idea what you've put her through these last couple of days? If she had any sense, she'd leave you and not put up with your crap anymore." It wasn't exactly the words I expected, but they were true. I looked over at my wife as the tears rolled down her face, and I told her I was sorry. She had heard me say that so many times before, and there was no reason to believe that this time was going to be any different. She smiled, however, and gave me a hug and kissed me. I thought for sure I wasn't going to be here; I wasn't prepared and wasn't sure what I was feeling. I hurt all the people I loved, and I didn't know what to say to make the hurt go away. I couldn't even say I would never do that again, even to comfort them in that moment.

God sometimes waits until we have messed up our lives so badly and we are in the absolute worst situation we have ever been in for God to come and pull us out. You see, for some of us, that's the only time we are willing to let God work in our lives. When we finally have messed things up so badly, we give up. That's what was happening to me.

Chapter Two — Opening My Eyes to Others

The hospital room I was in was for people who had to be watched around the clock because they suffered from severe neurological ailments. In that room was a young Marine who had been in there for two and a half months. One day, he was driving a truck on maneuvers; the steering failed, and the truck went up a hill and rolled over. As the truck rolled, he was thrown out of the cab, and the truck landed on his leg, arm, and head. He had been in that bed all that time without any emotional response except for cries from severe pain. He was being fed through a tube and could only have water by sucking on a sponge.

While the doctors were attending to me, my sister, who is a professional comedian, took the opportunity to perform for my new roommate. My sister did what she always does: treat everyone the same no matter what. She went over and asked what the heck he was doing, just lying around. His mother, who was sitting next to him, was unsure what to do and didn't say anything. She went around his bed and found things to poke fun at. She did a command performance to an audience of one, and it was one of her toughest. Kathy picked up the sponge that he used to moisten his mouth and asked if it was a giant Q-tip. She showed it to his mother and asked what the heck it was for, and his mother, while laughing now, explained that was how he drank. She said no wonder you're not getting better; you're dehydrated and proceeded to fire each nurse in the room along with the doctor who was caring for me.

The young man lying in bed started to smile.

His mother looked over and cried out, "He's smiling."

Kathy said, "Of course, this is funny stuff, and he tried to laugh."

His eyes were focused on Kathy, something he couldn't do, and the nurse rushed to his side. As the nurse was checking him, Kathy went to the opposite side of the bed and held his hand. His mother, in between her crying, said, "That's the first sign of any kind he's shown. Thank you so much for making him smile."

Kathy smiled and said, "Up until now, there was nothing to smile about," then kissed him on the forehead.

The young man's name was Tim, and he was one day older than my son, who was now in the Army. Gail, Tim's mother, told Kathy about the day the Marines called her in Connecticut to tell her about her son's accident. When Gail and her husband arrived, the doctor who was treating Tim told them they were keeping Tim alive with life support, and he wasn't going to make it. The chaplain of the Marines had conveyed the same message to them, but they refused to have him disconnected. A few days later, a miracle happened, and he started breathing on his own. Then the doctors told them his leg was shattered, he would never be able to walk on it, his throat was damaged, and he probably would never be able to speak. They were also told if he did survive, he may only have the mental capacity of a first or second-grader. Tim had been lying in that bed for two and a half months with his mother by his side, and the only thing she heard from him was the cry of pain until that night.

Kathy made her way back to me as the doctor was finishing up his examination. The doctor told my family that I was very lucky and that he wanted to do other tests to see if any of my organs may have been damaged by the overdose. I lay there as the three of them gave me a lecture and took turns calling me stupid, selfish, insensitive, and other descriptive words. I was still groggy, and my head was spinning as they each took their well-deserved shot. When they were finished, they told me how much they loved me, and the nurse told them it was time to leave.

Before Kathy left, she said, "Oh, by the way, Tim, this is my big stupid brother Mark, big stupid brother Mark, Tim."

I looked over and said, "Hi, Tim," but he never looked in my direction.

The next morning, about five o'clock, I woke up, and standing over me was an orderly. He was a big man and introduced himself as John. He told me I stunk and needed a shower before I smelled up the whole floor. I thanked him for his discretion and agreed it would be a good idea. I tried to sit up, but my back was so stiff I could barely do it. John helped me get to the shower, but I was still dizzy and not standing too well. He helped me get undressed and handed me soap and a washcloth. The water felt good, and my mind was beginning to clear up a little, which wasn't necessarily a good thing. I looked down toward my feet and noticed all the sand that was washing off my body. It was forming a mud puddle in the bottom of the shower. It took most of my concentration just to wash myself. When I was finished,

I began to dry myself when I heard John ask if I was okay. I told him I think I'll live. When I passed Tim's bed, I looked down at him and held his hand. I told him he was going to be all right. I don't know why I said it; it just came out suddenly, but I knew it was true. Tim didn't look up at me or make any indication that he heard me, but I felt he did.

When I returned to my bed, there was breakfast, and I uncovered it and told Tim his breakfast looked better than mine. Tim just lay there staring into space with a tube inserted in his stomach. For some reason, I kept talking to Tim as if he understood what I was saying. I told him about my son, who was now in the Army in Georgia, about my daughter and how she had just recently come out to California from Ohio. Periodically, the nurse in charge of our room would look up, hoping Tim would give some response. At one point, I said, "Well enough about me, tell me a little about you."

There was a moment of silence, and I said, "I see you're not much of a conversationalist." It was strange; while I was talking to Tim, I told him all about the good things in my life. I told him about my family, friends, and good things that had happened to me, things I should be thankful for. I normally didn't think of these things, but it felt natural to talk about them to him. The more I told Tim, the better I felt. When I was finished talking, I looked at Tim. There in the bed next to me was a young man fighting for his life, and here I was, trying to end mine. As I looked into his face, he turned his head and looked into my eyes. I looked back and smiled and again told him, "You're going to be all right, Tim. Hang in there."

As I was lying there staring at the ceiling, Gail, Tim's mom, said, "You have a very nice family." Gail sounded nervous as if she wasn't sure if it was okay to speak to me. I told her that they were very special. "I was talking to your wife," she said, "she told me why you were here. I hope you don't mind me asking, but why would you do something like that."

Her question surprised me, and I started to search for an answer. "It's difficult to explain," I told her as I stalled for time. As I tried to come up with a suitable answer, I discovered there was no logical explanation for what I did or the way I felt. I said to her, "Honesty, I really don't know. For most of my life, I felt depressed and hopeless. It doesn't seem to take much to trigger it; I just feel as if I don't have anything to live for."

Gail acted surprised and asked, "What about your family?" My family is terrific, but most of the time, I don't think about the good things in my life. While you were out to lunch with my wife and sister, I had a one-sided conversation with your son. I told Tim all about my life and all the wonderful things in it. Things I normally don't think of or thankful for." I smiled and said, "Tim is a good listener." I continued, "I look at Tim, and he reminds me of how good I have it; I can't imagine how hard this is on you. I don't know how well I would hold up having my son in the condition that Tim is in."

Gail looked over at Tim, started crying, and said, "I don't think that I'm holding up all that well." Gail then told me about all the things that had happened, how the Marine Corps wasn't helping Tim, and all the red tape they had put her through. She talked about the small house they had back in Connecticut and the financial burden they had. She talked while I listened as I thought of more and more things to be grateful for. When she was finished, she apologized for carrying on, and I told her I was glad she felt she could talk to me.

I then said, "To answer your question about why I would try to commit suicide."

Gail sat up, thinking she was going to hear great words of wisdom. "I feel it's because I'm selfish." Gail looked confused as I continued, "Most of my life, all I thought about was me and how everything depended on what I did. I realized I had no faith in myself, and if I couldn't depend on myself, why should others?"

She said, "Maybe all you need is more faith; it works for me."

I looked at her, smiled, and said, "I think you're right."

Just then, Tim cried out in pain and tried to grab his stomach, but his hands were tied down. He then started going into convulsions. The nurse ran over to calm him down and pushed the button for more help. His mother held his hand and told him that she was there. I looked at his face, distorted from the pain. I hurt just looking at him and feeling useless, but his mom continued to hold his hand, telling him he was going to be all right. She'd been going through this for two and a half months but still insisted he was going to be okay. I watched as they attempted to medicate him, to subdue the pain. I looked at his mother's face to see the love she had for her son. I asked God to help him and ease his pain, then asked what I could do to help. The pain started to subside as his body relaxed, and he laid his head back on the pillow. I looked over at his mother as she put her head down and sighed, "Thank you, God."

I lay there that evening after everyone had gone, looking at Tim, trying to imagine what he must be going through. Then I thought about my son in the Army and how this could have been him. How would I handle this situation if it were my son? Could I give myself totally to him and be there each day? I watched Tim as he would close his eyes and then open them quickly because of the pain. I saw a young man fighting for his life, and I felt inside of me wanting to help. I got out of my bed, went to his side, and knelt next to him. I whispered, "You can depend on me." I held his hand, and he turned his head and looked me in the eyes. His face, which was tense with pain, relaxed, and a calming look came over it. I kissed him on the forehead and said good night, then went back to my bed.

The next day, the doctor came in and said I would be released the next day and made an appointment with the doctor they wanted me to see. I said, "Great, I'm ready to get out of this place." As I said that, I happened to look over at Tim's mom, saw her put her head down, and then looked over and said, "I'm really going to miss you." I told her that she wasn't going to get rid of me that easily, "I plan on checking up on Tim a couple times a week."

She replied, "God must have sent you here for me."

I couldn't imagine God being able to use someone like me for anything.

The next morning, I gave Tim a cheerful "*Good Morning*" and told him he looked lovely. I sat down, held his hand, and explained to him that I was leaving, but I was going to visit. I told him he was important in my life, that I loved him, and that there wasn't anything I wouldn't do for him. These just weren't words but true feelings I felt in my heart. I looked him in the eyes, and he turned and looked into mine, and he squeezed my hand. I told him he had quite a grip, and the nurse stationed in the room asked if he squeezed my hand. I said, squeezed; he almost broke it as I smiled. She came over to the bed, and Tim was still holding onto my hand. She told me that was the first time he squeezed anyone's hand that wasn't related to pain. I looked at him and said I told you that you were going to be all right. I sat there with Tim for a while until Gail came in. The nurse gave her the good news about his hand squeezing, and you would have thought she told her that Tim was cured. Gail came over, gave me a hug, and thanked me. "I didn't do anything," I said.

"Well, someone did," she smiled. "It must be Tim. I think he's finally getting tired of this place, and he's ready to get out of here." I looked at Tim as I said it, hoping it was true.

I went back over to my bed to gather my things. I picked up the bag that my wife had brought my things in. It was a jean bag that my sister gave me from one of the awards shows she was on. On the bag was the saying, "Too tough to die." I took the rest of the things I had already packed out of the bag and gave them to Tim. I told him that the bag must be his, as I pointed out the saying on it. I handed it to Gail, and she thanked me and asked me if I was sure that it was okay. I told her, "It's more than okay." I sat there for a while and kept Gail company. When my wife arrived, Gail and I said our goodbyes while I said goodbye to Tim. As I was talking to him, a strange feeling came over me. For some reason, with all that was happening and uncertain in my life, I felt at peace. I left the room feeling better than I had for some time.

It was time to leave, and I had no idea what to do next. I knew we were behind in our bills, including rent. As I was about to feel sorry for myself, I began to think of Tim. I wondered if he was really going to be all right. I looked down at the hand Tim squeezed and smiled.

When I got home, I called both my parents, and each call ended with them saying, "As long as you're all right." Then I had to call Kathy; I was afraid to call, assuming she was going to give me another lecture. I gathered up my courage and dialed the phone. Kathy answered. I said, "Hello, I'm home."

She said, "Who is this?"

I said, "Very funny, it's your brother."

"Oh, my brother, Mark. How are you?" she said with a slight English accent.

"I'm doing pretty well. How are you?" I responded.

"That depends on whether you have any future plans to go to the beach."

"I'm not sure exactly what I'm going to do, but I do plan on being here for my family."

Then she gave me the lecture and told me about all the people that loved me, about how my life was connected to others, and that I had no right to treat my life with so little respect. At the end of the lecture, she told me that God made me for a reason. I wondered, after she said it, what could that reason possibly be? Before we hung up, she told me that she loved me and that it was time I took care of my family instead of my family taking care of me.

I told my wife I should probably call our son and let him know I was alright. She said, "I never told him what happened. There was no way he could come home, and it wouldn't do anyone any good if he did. I need to call him and tell him because he'll find out eventually." She decided to call him right then and explain what had happened.

My daughter, who was upstairs at that time, overheard the conversation and yelled down, "Don't call!" She came downstairs and said, "I called him this morning and told him what happened."

I asked, "How he took the news?"

She said, "He's very upset that no one called him when it happened."

I tried to explain that there wasn't anything I could do. I asked if I should call him, and she didn't think that it would be a good idea. My daughter, not able to keep her emotions bottled up, started to cry. Through the tears, she said, "How could you be so selfish. You're our father. How do you think this would affect us? You're not here for us anymore. Don't you care about seeing your grandchildren, didn't you care about us, and don't you care about me? I love you and depend on you. Your son is trying to make himself better by joining the Army. He joined so you would be proud of him. How did you think he was going to feel when he heard his father was dead because he didn't want to be with him anymore? Do you know what you did to mom? She loves you so much. What did you think that it was going to do to her?"

My daughter could barely breathe; she was yelling and crying so hard. My heart was broken, and I realized the pain I was putting my family through. She was standing over me, and I got down on my knees in front of her. With my head bowed down, I asked her to forgive me.

She said sternly, "You can't do this to us anymore. I can't stop loving you, Dad, and I can't take it anymore."

I begged her to forgive me, and I promised I would never do anything like that again. She kneeled down in front of me, hugged me, and told me she loved me. I held her tight and told her that I loved her. We held each other until we stopped crying.

When we all calmed down, she went back to her room. How was I going to straighten out this mess I made? I clasped my hands together and asked God, "What am I supposed to do now?" It was as if someone asked me the question, "What have you learned?" The question startled me as I searched for an answer. I guess I learned that my family loves me very much, depends on me, and that my life doesn't only affect me. Then I started to cry, "I should be thankful for the family I have." As I sat there and cried, a peace came over me. I felt completely exhausted, as if I couldn't stand. I had been so selfish. I had no idea what I had done to everyone else's life.

When they called my daughter and told her that I was in the hospital, she was with a young man she was only dating for a couple of weeks, Justin. Justin volunteered to take her to the hospital and sat outside the room while she was there with me. I'm not sure how long he waited for her, but knowing this young man, he would have been there for as long as it took. While I was sitting on the couch, Justin came up to me and handed me a book entitled *Prison to Praise*. He told me that maybe this book would be able to help me sort things out. I thanked him for the book and placed the book on the end table. This was one of the first times I met him, and yet he had the courage to approach this obviously troubled man and offer help.

The next morning, I sat down on the couch and looked over to see the book on the end table. I was never a good reader and rarely attempted to read a book. When I did try to read, my mind would wander, and I wouldn't remember what I read. However, I still picked up the book and began to read. The book opens with the author, Merlin Carothers, talking about his time in the army. Since my son was in the army, that drew my attention. After a couple of pages, he talked about being stationed in Fort Benning, Georgia, the same place where my son was stationed. Now, it really got my attention. I sat down that day and read the entire book.

The book described how thanking God changed his life. The book talked about Christianity, something I knew nothing about, and how he became a chaplain in the army, helping people. The main principle I received from the book was to thank God each day for everything you have in your life. The fact we are breathing and have the opportunity to improve our lives each day is a miracle. It spoke of putting the focus on God, not yourself, and to trust in God. All these ideas were new to me.

After I was finished reading, I knelt in front of the couch, put my hands together, and started thinking of things to thank God for. I started by thanking Him for my wife, my daughter, my son, and my sister. Then, I went on to thank God for my mother, father, brother, and friends. The more I thanked God, the more there was to be thankful for. Finally, after several minutes of thanking God, I got up and sat on the couch. I felt different; in fact, I felt pretty good. I put my shoes on and went for a walk with my dog. It was a beautiful day, so I thanked God for that. I looked down at my dog as she sniffed everything in sight, and I thanked God for her. I noticed things I had never noticed before, such as plants, small animals, and my neighbors working in a yard. Even the air smelled different, but I thanked God for everything that I noticed. Even with all the problems I had, at that moment, I felt better than I had felt in a long time.

The next day, I went back to the hospital to visit Tim. It seemed strange walking into the hospital, where I was wheeled out of a couple of days prior. I went up to Tim's room, and there was Gail in her regular seat sitting next to Tim. With a smile on my face, I asked how my ex-roommate was. I went over, gave Gail a hug and kiss on the cheek, then asked how she was doing. She looked so tired and said she was doing the best that she could. She asked how I was doing. I told her I was doing very well, which I was, for some reason. I asked how Tim was doing, and Gail said about the same, but she told me Tim had visitors. I asked Tim, who visited him, as if he could answer.

Gail told me some of his friends from the Marines and his sergeant came to visit him. Gail then showed me the things that they brought for Tim. I sat next to Tim, held his hand, and asked him how things were going. He squeezed my hand again and then looked over at me. Gail said, "That is so strange; you're the only person that he responds to."

I said, "That's because we were room buddies with Nurse Ratchet over there," as the nurse looked up and gave me a dirty look. "Just kidding," I said. She told me if I wasn't careful that, I would end up back in that bed. Gail said she had some things that needed to get done and asked if I would mind staying with Tim for a while. I told her to go ahead and take her time. After Gail left, I sat there and talked to Tim as if there was nothing wrong with him and that he understood everything I was saying. Tim arched his back in pain and started to cry out. The nurse and staff went to work, a regular routine, to ease Tim's suffering. When I was able to sit down next to Tim again, he was sleeping from all the medication they gave him. I sat there and told Tim all about my life and the uncertainty of my future. I told him again how I knew he was going to be all right and the new feelings I was experiencing. I brought a copy of Prison to Praise with me and started reading it.

I stopped to say, "I know you probably don't think you have anything to be thankful for, but there is if you only look." I looked around his bed and said, "You should be thankful for your mother, the friends you made in the Marines, that you're still alive, and all the blessings you have," and pointed to a picture of his girlfriend. I said, "I feel much better thinking about all the great things that God has given me." Did I just say, "That God had given me?" I thought about what I just said and started to cry. After all the terrible things I had done, why would God give me all these gifts, I thought. Something was happening to me, and I needed to know what it was.

Chapter Three — This Isn't the Church I'm Used To

That Sunday, Justin invited me to his church. I figured since I'd been talking to God each day, it was time to visit him at home. The only church I had ever attended before was a Catholic Church when I was young. Today, however, I was about to attend a Christian church. I had no idea what to expect, but I knew I was searching for something that was missing in my life, and this seemed as good a place as any to find it. As we pulled up to the church, several people were waving as we came in, so I waved back. We pulled into the parking lot, and again, people were directing us where to park and smiling and waving at us.

The church was a large building with a row of palm trees lining the walkway. It didn't look like a church; there were no steeple or church bells. We got out of the car and walked to the entrance of the church. People were smiling and shaking my hand to welcome me. I walked through the untraditional glass doors; the foyer looked just like any building with no crucifixes or stations of the cross, nothing indicating that it was a church. I walked into the sanctuary, and again, someone shook my hand and gave me a program. Walking inside, it looked more like an auditorium with white patio chairs instead of pews, and with the exception of a large sign over the stage reading Jesus, I thought I was in a theatre.

Off to the one side of the stage were musical instruments, microphones, and music stands. I sat down in my plastic chair while trying to get comfortable. I sat there confused about my surroundings and lack of religious artifacts. I watched as several musicians with saxophones, trumpets, clarinets, and guitars filled the area next to the stage, along with a drummer. Then, the choir marched on stage along with the group's conductor. I wasn't sure if I was in church or at a concert. I was ready to hear a slow gospel song with a solo done by a woman who could reach a note only my dogs could hear.

Then the music started; it had an upbeat tempo, and instantly, everyone stood and started to clap their hands. I began clapping, and the choir started to sing. There were two large television monitors on either side of the stage with the words of the song. I'm not a singer, but I do love to pretend. There were plenty of people singing, and I was sure they would be able to drown out my terrible voice, so I began to sing. The song was about Jesus, how he is with us, and how he is our brother and cares for us. The song went on to tell how he gave his life so our lives would be saved. They played a couple more songs and ended with a song called "Shout to the Lord." The woman who sang it was with such conviction that I was moved. The song was over, and the pastor came out screaming, "Let's hear it for the Lord," and started applauding while everyone was standing and clapping with him.

My first thoughts were about those television evangelists with the rhinestone jackets, asking for money and healing people on stage. He finally had everyone sit down and ask, "Isn't the Lord good?" People all over the sanctuary were either yelling yes or amen. This was definitely different from the church I was used to. He told everyone to get out their Bible. I had never owned a Bible and had only seen one in a motel room. I looked around, and it seemed as though everyone else had one. I felt as though I were back in school and had forgotten my books at home, ready for the teacher to notice I had forgotten.

The message that day was about how the devil can influence our thinking. He asked if we ever tell ourselves that we're no good or incapable of doing things right. He went on to say that the devil was the father of lies, and if we let him, he can lead us astray. The things he was saying and the way he was saying them made me feel as though he was talking to me. I had to look around to see if there was anyone else there. The pastor didn't give the message with fire and brimstone or shout, "*repent.*" He simply told of everyday occurrences that may happen to anyone and told humorous stories that related to his message. As he spoke, I thought about the way I looked at life and how I always put myself down and looked at the worst side of a situation. The idea of Satan causing some of the way I thought seemed far-fetched. As I thought about it, a feeling of hope came over me. The situations he talked about were situations that had happened to me, but I always thought they only happened to me. It was comforting to find out that I wasn't the only one.

The pastor said, "All the answers are written right here in the word," as he held up the Bible. He said, "Jesus had already won the fight against Satan, and if you let him, He will fight for each one of you."

I wanted to believe it, but it still seemed too strange for me. At the end of his message, he asked us to bow our heads in prayer. He gave a beautiful prayer, at the end of which he asked if anyone wanted to accept Jesus as their personal savior. I didn't know exactly what that meant, and I didn't feel as if I should raise my hand, so I sat there. After that, they took up the collection and sang one more song.

I was planning on going the following week but thought I should go out and purchase a bible before I went. The next day, I was sitting at my desk, and there lying on it was my new Bible. I took my Bible, went out on the patio, sat down, and began to read. I started at the beginning, but I didn't understand what was happening. I remembered that the pastor gave us notes with Bible verses to look up. I found my notes and started to look up different scriptures. I realized the version I had had notes on the bottom explaining certain passages. I spent most of that day reading different parts of the Bible, finding stories I had seen in movies like Moses, Samson, Delilah, David, and Goliath, and I realized Ben Hur wasn't actually in the Bible. When I went to bed that night, I prayed, thanking God for that day. I was turning into a praying machine two times in one day. Along with thanking Him, I asked him to show me what it was I was supposed to do. Something was happening to me, but I didn't know what it was or what I was supposed to do about it.

The next morning, I went and visited my buddy Tim. I was surprised when I arrived that Gail wasn't in her usual place, so I asked the nurse where she was. She told me that Gail had several meetings with officers of the Marines and Navy that day. I turned and told Tim it looked like it was going to be just the two of us today. Tim looked up and put his hand out. I reached out and grabbed his hand and told him he looked adorable. Tim forced a smile and opened his mouth a little, but nothing came out. I asked him if he wanted to play cards, Monopoly, Yahtzee, or maybe Twister. That brought a laugh from the nurse, but Tim started to drift away. I sat there and told Tim about my experience in church that week and that I felt different, but I couldn't explain it.

Suddenly, Tim arched his back and moaned out in pain. He tossed and turned, trying to get free from the restraints that were holding down his arms. The nurse immediately called for help, and in an instant, a couple of orderlies were there. I kept asking what I could do to help, and they just told me to get out of the way as they closed the curtain around him. I felt so helpless I didn't know what to do. The patient in the bed across from Tim told me, "He goes through this a couple of times a day. I pray for him and ask God to relieve his pain."

Now, people around me were talking about God and praying; I don't know if it was a coincidence or if I was just more sensitive and noticing it more. He asked, "Would you like to pray for Tim with me?" I was uncomfortable at first, but then I heard Tim cry out in pain again, and I agreed. He put his hands out and grabbed mine, and together we prayed. He asked God to heal Tim and to allow him to have peace. The man's voice was so mellow, and he prayed with great conviction, and then he stopped. I realized he was waiting for me to say something. I asked God that day to use me to help Tim get well. I tried to sound as eloquent as that kind man sounded, but it was obvious I was an amateur. He ended the prayer by repeating a verse from the book:

"Again, I tell you that if two of you on earth agree about anything you ask for, it will be done for you by my Father in heaven. [20] For where two or three come together in my name, there am I with them."

— **Matthew 18:19-20**

I thanked the man, and before I left, I told him, "I'll pray for you," something I wasn't accustomed to saying. He smiled, thanked me, and asked if I was the man who had been brought in a couple of weeks prior. I said, "Yes, have I become a legend?"

He said, "No, but I talked to Gail, and she has been very thankful for you, your wife, and I believe your sister." He asked how I was doing. I told him I was doing pretty well. Just then, the curtains were drawn back, and Tim was calm once again. I asked the nurse if there was anything I could do to help. She said if you don't mind, you could take a damp washcloth and wipe his face. I spent several hours with Tim that day, mostly watching him sleep. I borrowed a Bible from my new prayer partner and read while Tim slept. Gail came later that afternoon to relieve me. She was very thankful that I had stayed. I told her it was my pleasure, and it was.

The rest of the week, I made phone calls to find a permanent job, worked around the house, and read. It was a time I had never had before. Kathy called the next day to check up on me, as she had been doing. I told her I had a strange question for her, and she replied, "So what's new?"

I told her about my experiences in regard to the church, thanking God each day and praying at night. "It's about time," Kathy said. She asked me, "How do you think I'm able to speak in front of so many people? How do you think I survived everything I survived, and how do you think I'm able to help people? God has directed my life and has taken care of me all these years." She then told me about the day that she found out I took the overdose. She said, "I was so mad at God for letting this happen that I yelled, how could you let this happen to my brother. As I was lying there crying, I heard a voice say, why are you crying? He's still alive, isn't he? God isn't finished with you yet." Kathy told me about situations that she had been in that only God could have gotten her out of and about all the gifts He had given her. Before she hung up, she said, "Be patient and watch God work in your life." It was as if everyone else knew about God but me.

Then came Sunday and time to go to church. This time, I waved back to the people standing on the corner and in the parking lot. I took my seat right before the music began. After a couple of songs, they announced, "Turn to five people around you and welcome them to the church." I always hated shaking hands with strangers. I turned around pretending I was shaking hands, but in this church, people were determined to shake your hand, and they didn't look down when they approached you. One woman even came up and gave me a hug.

The pastor came out, as he did before, yelling and clapping for Jesus. The man was so full of energy that some of it spilled over onto you as you watched him. This week's message was about the burdens we all carry around with us. He talked about the burdens of guilt, pride, jealousy, past experiences, desire to impress others, and the list went on. He talked about the burden of the past and how, no matter what we do, we take that burden with us wherever we go. He talked about how that burden continually grows since we never throw any of it away, and we keep adding to it.

Then he really hit home when he said, "The burden can grow into depression, and some of us may get to a place where we feel ending our life is the only way out." He went on to say that some of us can't enjoy our lives because we feel there is no present, only the bad memories of the past and the worries of tomorrow. As he was speaking, I wanted to cry out loud. My body was shaking, and it took everything to hold back the tears. I couldn't even look up at him as he spoke; I sat there with my head down, looking at the back of the chair in front of me.

He went on to say, "Life is right now, this moment, and as soon as I speak, it's already in the past, and nothing I can do will change that. The past is history, tomorrow is a mystery, and right now is a gift. That's why it's called the present." Then he asked, "Do you want to know how to get rid of your burdens?" I almost stood up right there and yelled, yes. He said, "Give them to God, he wants them. He loves us so much that he was ridiculed, beaten, tortured, and died for our sins so that we may have peace. Take your burdens and lay them at the foot of the cross. He doesn't just want you to give your burdens to Him; He commands it."

"I have told you these things so that in me you may have peace. In this world, you will have trouble. But take heart! I have overcome the world."

— John 16:33

He then said, "Thank God for all your blessings and ask him to take your burdens and make them into blessings." I thought to myself, "I've been thanking God for what he has given me, and that has already helped me. I don't know how he could take the past bitter memories and make them a blessing, but I was willing to ask Him." That day after the message, he asked again for us to bow our heads as he prayed. When he came to the part and asked, "Who wants to have a personal relationship with Jesus? Who believes that Jesus rose from the dead so that we may have life everlasting? Raise your hand so we may pray for you." I raised my hand right away as high as I could with my hand up and head down. I felt a chill come over my body, and I began to cry. Not tears of sadness but tears of joy, and I didn't care who saw me.

When the service was just about over, the Pastor said, "Anyone who made a decision for Christ, there will be prayer partners to pray with you." I went up after service, my eyes still red from crying and my body shaking. We met with one of the pastors there in front of the stage, and I told him I wanted to do what was right. He smiled at me and gave me a hug. I couldn't believe I was doing this, something I would have thought bizarre and would have probably mocked. We prayed together, and at the end of the prayer, he told me I was now born again. What a terrific thought it was to be born again. It's a chance to do it all over, but this time, do it right.

I left the church that day feeling different, with hope and joy. I couldn't explain it and didn't care to; I just wanted to enjoy it. I spent the rest of that day walking around the neighborhood, over to a nearby park, and watching the children play. I took time to read the Bible, visit with God, relax, and enjoy my new birthday.

I received Jesus as my Lord and Savior and was looking forward to seeing Tim the next day. When I got to Tim's room, his mom was sitting at her regular spot. I smiled and cheerfully asked her how she was doing. She said fine, but the expression on her face told me she wasn't. Then I turned to Tim and said, "Hi Tim. How's it going?"

He looked at me, and instead of putting his hand out today, he said, "Hi, Mark." I almost fell on the floor, and if his mom hadn't been sitting down, I'm sure she would have. The nurse stood up at her desk and asked if he talked.

"Yes," I said like a proud father whose baby just said daddy, "He said, 'Hi, Mark.'"

Tim looked at me and smiled. I got on my knees next to him. I knelt there saying, "Thank you, thank you, dear God." As I prayed, Tim reached over with his hand and held mine. I held his with both my hands and told him I loved him and that he was going to be all right. A gurney rolled into the room just then to take Tim down for more tests and therapy. The nurse told the orderly that Tim had talked.

The orderly, surprised and excited, said, "All right, Tim," but Tim just lay there as he'd been doing.

"I guess you're all talked out for now," he said. They lifted him up on the gurney as Tim cried out in pain.

I went over to him and said, "Everything is going to be okay, just as I told you the first time I met you." I can still hear Tim's voice in my ear, "Hi, Mark." I never realized how wonderful my name sounded. It was as if God was saying, "Hi, Mark! Welcome to the family."

The weeks went by, and Tim was constantly showing improvement. Gail would always tell me that I was the only person Tim remembered. Tim was getting to the point where he could carry on a conversation but for only a short period. He was beginning to remember things back home as Gail would show him some old pictures.

When Tim arrived at the hospital a little over five months prior to my last visit, they told his mom he was going to die. Many people told Tim that he wasn't going to be able to do things, and he proved them wrong. Yet he still wasn't sure what he was going to be able to do. I was there the day they removed his feeding tube and gave him something to eat for the first time. Tim was my hero, the young man God chose to help me, and then God used me to help him.

I went home one night and made a card for Tim. I scanned a picture that was taken of Tim and me. I placed it on the front of the card with the words, "To Tim, the great explorer. I will be following your journey as you progress and hope to see you at its conclusion." I wrote the card so fast I had to wait until I was finished to read it:

Life Is Basic

Remember when you first joined the Marines, and they told you how many push-ups you were going to do? You said to yourself, "I can't do that."

But you did.

Then they told you how many miles you were going to run with a full-field pack.

And you said to yourself, "I can't do that."

But you did.

Then they told you all the things you must accomplish to pass the basics.

And you said to yourself, "I can't do that."

But you did.

Then, one day, you woke up in a hospital, unable to talk. And the doctors told you you'll never be able to talk.

But you did.

Now you lay here, hardly able to move. And think, you'll never be able to walk.

But you will.

You lay here confused and unable to think clearly. And say to yourself, I'll never be smart.

But you will.

All great explorers will take the toughest path, the path less traveled. They know by taking that path, they will learn and discover things they would never have been able to discover anywhere else. They discover feelings they never knew they had. They will see things in a different way. Even though this journey will take longer than if they had taken the path most traveled, when they return, they will tell others about their adventure so others can learn and become stronger in their knowledge.

Tim, you are one of these great explorers. By fate, you are traveling on a path only a few have taken. A path that is full of pain and confusion. A long journey that can only be completed by will and faith. As you look back on all the things in your life that you felt you could not do but did, this journey will be just one more accomplishment.

I know you will fulfill your life's journey. For you see, you have a Guide who knows the path you are on. Listen to Him with all your heart. Follow His direction and never give up hope. Draw strength from His love and the love around you. When you finish your journey, reach out and tell others so they can become stronger in their knowledge.

Something I was never very good at was writing, but I didn't feel as if I wrote this that night. I sat there and watched someone else do it using my hand. When I stopped and read what was written, I got down on my knees and cried as I felt a special chill come over my body again.

The next day, I went to the hospital to give Tim the card. When I arrived, Tim had company from some of the Marines he was stationed with. Tim looked uneasy and tried to smile when one of the guys was telling him a joke. I could tell that his friends felt uncomfortable around Tim, seeing him lying there now weighing under a hundred pounds. Tim's mom saw me and came over and gave me a hug. I walked in and said that maybe I should have made a reservation to get in there. Tim's spirits picked up when he saw me and said, "Hi, Mark." I asked him how it was going, and he told me pretty good. I told Tim I would come back later so he could visit with his friends.

One of his friends spoke up right away and said, "We have to be going now."

I said to Gail, "If you would like to go out for some lunch, I'll stay here and aggravate Tim."

Tim spoke up in his raspy voice and said that sounded good to him. His buddies then all shook his hands and left with Gail right behind them. I sat down and said to Tim, "It must have been nice to see all your friends."

He looked down and said, "I don't remember any of them; they don't even look familiar." I held his hand and told him, "Maybe that's a part of your life you're not supposed to remember because of the pain attached to it. You've been through a lot, and you're very fortunate to be in as good of shape as you are. God must really love you to take such good care of you."

Tim looked at me and said, "If God loves me, why did he let this happen to me?"

I told him, "I don't know why God does the things He does, and we don't need to know. I know now that everything happens for a reason, and if we focus on the good that can come out of it, we'll be focusing on God." I sat there, not believing what I was saying. I, Mr. Depression, was giving advice on focusing on the good. Will the miracles ever cease?

Tim said, "What good could possibly come out of this?"

"You'll be going home soon to see your family. You should be taken care of, giving you time to do things that you would want to do and have time to go to college."

I said, "We were able to meet and become friends." I told Tim how much he meant to me, being in my life, and how he has helped me. I told him, "I have never thought about someone more than I think about myself, and you have been in my thoughts and prayers continually."

Tim looked up at me, and I bent over to give him a hug. I told him I had made something for him and gave him the card I had made. He opened it and saw the picture on the front, then began to laugh. He read the front of the card, which surprised me because I didn't realize he was able to read yet. I was so happy he could read.

I hugged him again; he looked at me and said, "What do you think? I'm some kind of a dummy?"

I said, "I'm sorry, Einstein, please continue," and we both laughed. I sat there while he read the card, trying to calm my emotions. I felt like listening to him read the words I wrote. As he continued to read, his voice began to break up, trying to hold back his tears. When he finally finished, we both broke down and began to cry, then held each other. As I was hugging Tim, I heard someone else crying. I turned to see the nurse who was stationed in the room, crying and holding out a box of tissues. At that moment, Gail returned from lunch in time to see the three of us together, wiping our tears and blowing our noses.

"What's going on," Gail asked.

I told her, "We just saw the hospital bill," and the three of us started to laugh.

Tim held out the card and said to Gail, "See what Mark made me." After Gail read it, we passed the tissues to her.

Gail said, "We will be leaving tomorrow on a military plane that is set up like a hospital. It's going to take us several days to get back to Connecticut."

I told Tim, "I'm going to be out of town tomorrow. I will always stay in touch, and someday we'll see each other again. When you get sick of the cold and snow, come down and stay with me." I said goodbye to Gail, as she kept thanking me and telling me how much she would miss me. It hurt to say goodbye, but it felt good that he was getting better and going back home. Before I left, I looked at him and said, "I told you that you were going to be all right."

He said, "How did you know?"

I said, "God told me the first time I saw you."

Tim continued to get better. The boy who wouldn't be able to walk limped to a wheelchair, wouldn't be able to talk, said good-bye, and wouldn't have more than a first-grade mentality planned on going back to school.

Chapter Four — Time to Serve

I've talked to so many Christians about the change in their lives that happened when they received Jesus as Lord and Savior, and each one had something different that changed within them. I remember one of the first things that happened was I couldn't swear anymore, and when I heard God's name used in vain, I would get a sharp pain in my heart. But the one thing that really changed was the way I looked at people. I rarely even noticed or cared about them at all. I was so wrapped up in my own life, but now things were different. The homeless were no longer disgusting to me but unfortunate. The elderly were no longer just someone I needed to pass on the road, and children were not a bother but a blessing.

I started using my gift of food service to help organize the food service at church. I would work in what was called *The Garden of Eatin'* as a partner. I helped set up a patio area with a grill and steam table to serve food before and after services. I was on the committees for any large functions the church might be having, such as the

Thanksgiving dinner for the poor, Autumnfest, which was an alternative to Halloween, and the Sunrise service for Easter. For most of my life, I couldn't find anything useful for me, but God always knew I would come in handy.

What my God did for me was a series of miracles, one right after another. I compare God's love to professional wrestling. Wait, give me a moment to explain. Have you ever seen tag team wrestling? It's when there are two people on a team; one is in the ring fighting, and when he gets in trouble, he reaches out to touch the other one so he can come in and take over. All they need to do is reach out, and their partner jumps right in. Somehow, that selfish prayer of mine that day at the beach was close enough to make contact that my savior jumped in to save me. God was going to show me that He doesn't make mistakes. Everything He creates is for a purpose. He used several people to get the message to me. He took the focus I had on myself and aimed it toward others who needed me, and He brought other people into my life to guide me. One thing I did when I was so badly depressed was keep everyone out of my life. Have you ever done that? It seems that when you need people the most, you turn your back on them and don't want them around. One of God's greatest gifts is companionship and fellowship with each other. How many times does our Lord reference in His Word about loving each other and helping each other?

"A new command I give you: Love one another. As I have loved you, so you must love one another. By this, all men will know that you are my disciples if you love one another."

— John 13:34-35

"Love must be sincere. Hate what is evil; cling to what is good. Be devoted to one another in brotherly love. Honor one another above yourselves."

— Romans 12:9-10

"Now that you have purified yourselves by obeying the truth so that you have sincere love for your brothers, love one another deeply, from the heart."

— 1Peter 1:22

"Dear friends, since God so loved us, we also ought to love one another. No one has ever seen God, but if we love one another, God lives in us, and his love is made complete in us."

— 1 John 4:11-12

He didn't create us to handle this life alone; we can't. We need God to intercede, and then He blesses us with people around us.

It's been over twenty years since the Lord led me to Him. I'll never forget the day I sat in that chair and raised my hand to give my life to my savior, Jesus. God used so many people to lead me in the right direction, and I have been free from all medication even after I was told I would be under a doctor's care and on medication for the rest of my life.

So how did He do it? He helped me take the focus off me. He took the burdens I carried all my life; He lightened my load and gave my life meaning and purpose. He put the Holy Spirit within me and changed me as it says:

"Therefore, if anyone is in Christ, he is a new creation; the old has gone, the new has come!"

— 2 Corinthians 5:17

I lived by the beach in a small apartment, and I started working early so I could get up at 2 in the morning, walk along the beach, and pray. I noticed so many homeless people sleeping on the park benches, and my heart went out to them. Each week, I would purchase several gift cards to the nearby Dairy Queen and place them in a card I made that had the text on the front:

"Trust in the LORD with all your heart and lean not on your own understanding; in all your ways acknowledge him, and he will make your paths straight."

— **Proverbs 3:5-6**

"For God so loved the world that he gave his one and only Son, that whoever believes in him shall not perish but have eternal life."

— **John 3:16**

On the inside were the words: "May God continue to bless you and keep you safe, for He cares and loves you."

While the people were sleeping, I placed the card next to them and quietly left. I would volunteer to help feed the poor and homeless and lead the Thanksgiving Dinner at the church. One day, I was going through a very tough time in my life and had no direction on what God wanted me to do. I was heading for work when I saw this one homeless man who stood at the corner, walking toward the tracks where he slept. It was Sunday and early, so there was no traffic on the road, and God put on my heart to stop and give him some money. Like Jonah, I didn't want to stop and make excuses like I was going the opposite way and there was no way to turn around. I have my own problems, and I was running late.

One thing I learned is that God doesn't see our problems the same way we do, and He had me turn around. I stopped and looked in my wallet, and I had a twenty and a one-dollar bill in my pocket. I looked up to see which one He wanted me to give as if I didn't know. I ran over to the man and got his attention. I said I felt I was supposed to give this to you. Pretty heartfelt, don't you think? As I handed the money to him, I began to walk away.

He stopped me and said, "What's your name?"

Startled, I turned around and said, "I'm sorry, my name is Mark."

The man looked at me and said, "Wow, that's my name too."

As I looked into his face for the first time, I noticed his eyes were this bright blue and his toothless smile warming as he said thank you. I did say God bless you as I left. I walked back to my car, wondering what had just happened, and realized my anxiety was gone, and I proceeded to go to work. I never saw Mark again, but I'll never forget him.

"Do not forget to entertain strangers, for by so doing, some people have entertained angels without knowing it."

Time to Serve

I remember when I would take a test in school, at times, there would be a bonus question or something you could do for extra credit. Unfortunately, some Christians consider service as extra credit instead of the test itself. Our faith is reflected in what we do with what God has blessed us with.

"What does it profit, my brethren, if someone says he has faith but does not have works? Can faith save him? If a brother or sister is naked and destitute of daily food, and one of you says to them, 'Depart in peace, be warmed and filled,' but you do not give them the things that are needed for the body, what does it profit? Thus also, faith by itself, if it does not have works, is dead. But someone will say, 'You have faith, and I have works.' Show me your faith without your works, and I will show you my faith by my works."

— **James 2:14-18**

God makes it easy for us to do the works He calls us to do. He already has them set up for us; He's created us to do them. God gives us the passion to accomplish our tasks, and all we have to do is walk to them.

"For by grace you have been saved through faith, and that not of yourselves; it is the gift of God, not of works, lest anyone

should boast. For we are His workmanship, created in Christ Jesus for good works, which God prepared beforehand that we should walk in them."

— **Ephesians 2:8-10**

- What does our Lord and Savior say about service?

"Yet it shall not be so among you, but whoever desires to become great among you, let him be your servant. And whoever desires to be first among you, let him be your slave — just as the Son of Man did not come to be served, but to serve, and to give His life a ransom for many."

— **Matthew 20:26-28**

- What is the most important commandment?

"Jesus said to him, 'You shall love the LORD your God with all your heart, with all your soul, and with all your mind.'"

— **Matthew 22:37**

- What do we have to have to please God?

"But without faith, it is impossible to please Him, for he who comes to God must believe that He is and that He is a rewarder of those who diligently seek Him."

— **Hebrews 11:6**

Just a quick recap: Faith is demonstrated by the works we do, God has already planned what we are supposed to be doing, Jesus places service on the top of the list of things we are to be doing, the most important commandment is to love God totally, but we can't do that without faith, which is proven by works. It seems clear that we are here to do something, isn't it?

"He is a rewarder of those who diligently seek Him."

— Hebrews

Everything that God has given us is a gift, but the rewards for service to Him by serving others are our paycheck that will be cashed when we finally get home. I've had people ask me why we don't just go to Heaven once we are saved since we can't lose our salvation. The day we are saved is our first day on the job, and we don't retire from that job until it's time to go home. At church a while ago, the pastor introduced several people who were going on a mission trip to Africa. The congregation applauded them and sat right back down in their seat, along with me. I thought Christianity was not a spectator sport, but when we received Jesus as our Lord, we were drafted to play. God gave us the gifts, talents, and testimony to play our position, and we need to be ready to get into the game.

Getting Over Depression

I remember when I received Jesus at age 46, the first thing God placed on my heart was that I needed to be doing something. You must remember this was a guy before Jesus that didn't do anything for anyone, including my family. I was self-centered, and the only person I served was me, so this was a big revelation in my life. If you're a Christian, it's time to punch in and collect your paycheck. This is the only place and time we can earn the wages God has put aside for us. Once we're home, our place in heaven will be established from what we do for Christ here on earth. Don't get short paid but:

"Do not lay up for yourselves treasures on earth, where moth and rust destroy and where thieves break in and steal; but lay up for yourselves treasures in heaven, where neither moth nor rust destroys and where thieves do not break in and steal. For where your treasure is, there your heart will be also."

— Matthew 6:19-21

I was involved in a couple of small church groups, and one of the men in the group owned a nursing home. We thought it would be great to prepare a dinner and then show a movie one evening. Some of the men brought their children to help serve. We all showed up early, and the people were anxious to talk with us. I talked to a man who won the PGA Golf Tournament in 1968, and my friend found Freddy, who used to box and knew Rocky Graciano. Freddy had a hunchback, and my friend was over six foot five, but Freddy stood firm and occasionally gave him a jab to his stomach. I watched as the kids took the orders after everyone was seated; our guests ordered shrimp and filet mignon when we only had burgers and hot dogs. However, that day was a banquet of love.

After dinner, we set up the movie on a large screen. It was called *Joshua*, a Christian movie about a modern-day Jesus. I remember one part of the movie where a lady was addressing something one of the actors said and yelled out, "You can say that again." The gentleman sitting next to her said, "I didn't say anything," and the two went on for a couple of minutes, going back and forth about who said what. Yet it didn't disturb anyone else. They appeared to be used to it, but it made me laugh so hard that it hurt. At the end of the movie, Freddy came up to me with tears in his eyes. I know what it meant, and I hugged him with tears in my eyes and an indescribable, wonderful feeling in my spirit.

As I was getting things together to leave, a woman came up to me and said, "I know who sent you."

I looked at her and said, "You do, do you." She just looked at me. I looked back and said, "I love Him so much."

She said, "It shows," and gave me a big hug. I never truly loved anyone or anything my entire life, and now I love someone so much that it shows. What a change!

I then got involved in the CARE (Child Abuse Recovery Education) ministry for abused children. The church would host events at the church, inviting different agencies to bring kids. I hardly spent any time with my own children, and now God wanted me to be involved with children going through the worst kind of abuse. They needed a Santa for the Christmas party being held, and I stepped up to the challenge. The children have been so abused that no one was allowed to hug them because they were afraid of people. Everyone except for Santa. That day, I had everyone sitting on my lap, from small children to mothers going through substance abuse, seeing their children maybe for the first time in months. I was laughing and hugging everyone. It was as if I was born to do this. Maybe I was.

As I would reach out for children, placing them on my knee and asking what they wanted, I saw a little boy in line about four or five. He had burn marks all over his face, and it seemed as though someone tried to burn the freckles off with a cigarette. I was afraid to reach out to him, so I said from a distance, "What would you like for Christmas, little boy?"

He looked up at me and said, "I want a hug, Santa."

I couldn't hold back my tears, so I reached out to him and just held him in my arms as he embraced me. His name was Mikey, and I asked him to help me pass out the candy and toys to the other boys and girls. He was so excited and stuck by his new best friend, Santa, for the rest of the day. When it was time to go home, he ran up to me, gave me a big hug, and told me that he loved me. I took off my gloves and glasses and handed them to him, then said, "Santa loves you too, Merry Christmas," as he got on the bus. I don't know if Mikey will remember that day, but I sure know Santa will never forget.

Another year, as I played Santa, I overheard a woman tell one of my elves thank you for making me feel normal. She was excited to be there and asked if she could take a picture with Santa? I looked up and said, "Hello, little girl! What would you like for Christmas?"

She told me that she wanted to see her children, whom she hadn't seen for months, but they didn't make it to the party that day. We went to take a picture, and she gave me a big smile and thanked me. As I was finishing up, I saw her look at her picture, and she became sad. She asked if she could take another picture, but this time, she didn't smile. I got up while she was comparing her pictures and noticed that she was missing most of her back teeth, and you could notice it when she smiled. I asked if I could see the pictures, and I told her I thought she had a beautiful smile. She asked if she could hug Santa, and I said that is why I'm here.

The other wonderful thing about playing Santa was before lunch was served, I got to share the real reason for Christmas and ask if anyone wanted to receive Jesus as their Lord and Savior. I had everyone close their eyes, and if they wanted to receive Jesus, to raise their hands. As I looked around the room with my hands raised, I saw the woman, and as soon as I saw her, she looked up and smiled. I was right; that was one of the most beautiful smiles I had ever seen.

I'm Santa every year, and God has used me to touch people's hearts, from praying with moms sitting on my lap while others wait in line to encourage ladies that God has a plan for their lives.

I became a leader for children with autism at the church. It was a class held on Saturday night, and I was the only man who volunteered. I remember one night, as the parents were picking up their children, this one lady had two sons, and they were about to leave. I shouted, "Hey, what about me?" The two turned, wrapped their arms around me, and kissed me on the cheek. I looked up, and there was their mom with tears in her eyes.

She said, "Thank you for showing my boys some love." I found out that most children with autism usually only have a mother because the father can't take the pressure of dealing with a child with autism. Imagine God used someone who couldn't love anyone, even himself, to show love to those who need it.

I remember the one day that I spent with Jesus. I've been thinking a lot about Heaven, and the one thing that I look forward to above everything else is seeing Jesus. There have been times on this earth that I've felt closer to Jesus than others, but there was one day I felt as if I could reach out and touch Him. It was several years ago, and we were going to do a special dinner for the lady's ministry. It started out to be 300 and ended up having over 550 guests. I decided I was going to take off work that day and prepare all the food. The menu was wild rice stuffed chicken breast with a Marsala mushroom sauce, fresh salmon with a lemon caper glaze, and prime rib with fresh green beans, pasta primavera, and rosemary potatoes as accompaniments.

The day came, and I got up early to start. The day had its trials. First, I timed myself making just one stuffed chicken breast, and after my calculations, it would take all day just to do that. The local health inspector showed up because he had complaints about the food service at the church and needed to do an inspection. No one told me the oven, which I needed to use for the prime rib, was broken, and no matter what temperature it was set at, it went as high as it could go. However, I started the day knowing that my Lord wanted me to do this, and He knew there was no way I could do it alone, so He signed up as my sous-chef. From the beginning, He was there working right alongside me; we sang worship songs, and I must have talked His ear off as I rambled on. When I was doing the chicken breast, it was as if He had stopped time, and I finished way before I thought I could possibly have. We ended up talking to the health inspector and told him what we were doing. We had an opportunity to share my testimony and my love for God.

Everything checked out fine, and he was on his way. I had the prime rib in the oven for only half an hour when

I saw the smoke and turned off the oven. It looked a little charred, and I just let it sit in the oven until I could free up some other oven space. This is where Jesus showed off; before I placed the prime rib in the other oven, I checked the temperature, and it was just right. When we served the prime rib at the dinner, it was perfect. I'd never made prime rib as well as it turned out that night. The men who were serving that night, a little over fifty of them, started arriving about four.

I was blessed with a couple brothers who had experience in food service, and they took over the dining room and led the rest of the men, freeing me up to stay in the kitchen. Everything turned out great. When the men took the food to the sanctuary, where the dinner was being served, I found a quiet place outside behind the building. I fell to my knees, prayed, and thanked my Lord for an awesome day and for allowing everything to turn out so well. I broke down and cried and told Him how much I loved Him. That's when I felt His arm around my shoulders, and it felt like He drew me close to Him; then He lifted me up to my feet, and we walked to the sanctuary where dinner was being served. This was the first time I saw the sanctuary set up for this dinner, and it was beautiful. What made the evening even more special was several ladies were invited from shelters for abused women.

These women, who only knew of men to be abusive, were humbly served by godly men whose only objective was to please them. They had the opportunity to sit and talk with other women who showed the love of God to them. What a special evening that must have been for them. I saw my wife from a distance talking to the ladies at her table, and she was having so much fun; I love to see her laugh. Everything was under control, so we headed back to the kitchen to start cleaning up the mess. About halfway there, I felt His strong carpenter's arm around my shoulders again, and it felt like He said, "This was great; we need to do this again." He left me to finish cleaning up, but what a glorious day it was.

My wife and I took a mission trip to Mexico, where they gave out about 500 pairs of shoes, had games for the children, and oversaw the food, of course. We made 1,000 burritos, not in a kitchen but on a dirt road. In this community, the houses are a couple pieces of plywood; even the church has old tires, plywood, and a tarp for a roof. I used to worry about doing large events, but not anymore because I know He'll be there. "We get to do it again," His word tells me that He came to serve, and serve he does. How can you not love Him?

God blessed me with so much joy from serving; I wanted to help others experience that same joy. I started a ministry called the C.I.A. (Christians In Action) and came up with a booklet with over one hundred ways we can bless others by serving. The idea was to help others realize their purpose by supporting them in whatever outreach God might have put on their heart. Most of the outreaches I did had something to do with food since that is my gift. One year, we had a military outreach Christmas party. We invited families whose spouses were deployed or might return right before the event. We called and asked for specific gifts for the children, we had volunteers do crafts, take pictures with Santa (guess who was Santa), and have a wonderful lunch buffet.

We had a request from the wife of a soldier. He was praying that somehow his family would be able to go to Disneyland on Christmas day so the family wouldn't miss him not being there. It would be his wife and three children. With the generosity of the church, we were able to purchase all the gifts along with four tickets to Disneyland.

Getting Over Depression

It was a wonderful day as our guests were greeted and then directed to the crafts and pictures with Santa. We had over two hundred attendees, and I had a great time asking the children what they wanted and hugging each one. A little girl about five years old came and sat on my lap, and when I asked what she wanted, she said she wanted her daddy home. I told her that was beyond what Santa could deliver, but I knew of someone who could watch over him until He got home. I asked her if she knew Jesus, and with a smile, she said, "Yes." I asked her if she wanted to pray together to make sure her daddy gets home safely, and she hugged me and said, please. We sat there talking with Jesus, asking for a safe return for her dad as others waited their turn.

Right before lunch, I gathered everyone together and told them about the real gift of Christmas and the reason we were there that day: to celebrate the birth of our Savior. Santa excused himself and went right to the kitchen and changed out of his Santa jacket to his chef coat. After lunch, I went into the kitchen to clean up while the others called out names to receive their special gift. Someone came back to tell me there was someone who wanted to talk to me. It was the lady and three children who received the

Disneyland tickets. They took turns hugging and thanking me, but I insisted it wasn't me they should be thanking.

The mom gave me one last hug and said, "You made our Christmas."

I said, "No, you made mine. That moment was my Christmas, the one moment I'll remember most from that year."

How can it be so rewarding to put the needs of others above our own? All I ever thought of was myself. I couldn't care less about anyone else, and I was miserable. God commands us to put the needs of others above our own, and He is always looking out for our best interests. I guess if it was good enough for Jesus.

"For even the Son of Man did not come to be served, but to serve, and to give His life a ransom for many."

— Mark 10:45

Chapter Five — The Power of Your Testimony

We are still here in this fallen world, so what are we supposed to be doing? Jesus made it clear in the following:

"Therefore go and make disciples of all nations, baptizing them in the name of the Father and of the Son and of the Holy Spirit, and teaching them to obey everything I have commanded you. And surely I am with you always, to the very end of the age."

— Matthew 28:19-20

We are to go out and tell others about Jesus.

"However, Jesus did not permit him, but said to him, 'Go home to your friends, and tell them what great things the Lord has done for you, and how He has had compassion on you.'"

— Mark 5:19

That's how much God loves us, and now He wants to use us to help bring the rest of His children to Him. Each one of us will do it in a different way by using the gifts and abilities that God has given us. God will also arrange situations to put us next to those He wants us to tell. One of the gifts we will use is our testimony. Most people won't

73

go to church to hear about Jesus but will listen to what He has done in your life. Paul says it best in the following:

"Praise be to the God and Father of our Lord Jesus Christ, the Father of compassion and the God of all comfort, who comforts us in all our troubles so that we can comfort those in any trouble with the comfort we ourselves have received from God. For just as the sufferings of Christ flow over into our lives, so also through Christ our comfort overflows. If we are distressed, it is for your comfort and salvation; if we are comforted, it is for your comfort, which produces in you patient endurance of the same sufferings we suffer. And our hope for you is firm because we know that just as you share in our sufferings, so also you share in our comfort."

— Corinthians 1:3-7

People will relate to other people who have gone through what they are going through. If you suffer from drug addiction, you are more likely to listen to someone who suffers from the same addiction. Our testimony can be our most powerful witnessing tool; I know it is for me. There are certain people out there who might only hear about the gospel because of who you are and what you have gone through. We will not always see the harvest, but we may be the one who plants the seed or the one who waters it instead of reaping the reward of seeing someone receive Jesus as Lord and Savior. I've talked to a lot of people and given out hundreds of books, and it won't be until I get to heaven that I'll see the harvest that God has allowed me to be part of. However, there have been a few times that God has allowed me to see the planting and the harvest, and what a blessing it was.

The first time I spoke was in the church where I received Jesus as my Lord and Savior. After I had finished, I looked out over at the congregation as they applauded the message. People were crying and smiling back, and I saw how God used me to touch them. The chill was throughout my whole body as I walked toward the pastor and handed him the microphone. As I went back to the room behind the stage, one of the other pastors came back and gave me a hug. He told me to look out the small window that overlooked the sanctuary. He said the pastor is going to ask if anyone would like to dedicate his or her life to Christ, and you can see how God used you today. I went to the window and looked out as the Pastor asked the question. Hands started going up all over the sanctuary, and as each hand went up, my heart lifted up higher and higher. After the prayer, the pastor told me to make my way to the back of the sanctuary and greet the people as they left.

The people started coming through as they shook my hand or hugged me and thanked me for sharing. A woman came up to me, still with tears in her eyes, and gave me a hug. "I wish my husband were here today to hear your testimony," she said. Taking a deep breath, she went on saying he committed suicide six months ago; he was suffering from depression. I think if he heard what you said today, he might still be here, as she started to cry again. I felt helpless as I held her in my arms. I just wanted her pain to go away. A young pregnant woman then came up with tears in her eyes. "Thank you, thank you," she said and gave me a huge hug. The father of my baby was here with me today, and he suffers from depression; he told me he didn't think that he was going to live long enough to see the baby. You touched his heart and began to cry, holding my hand. Just then, the man came up with sunglasses on. He took the glasses off, and his eyes were red and puffy from crying. As soon as he saw me, he started crying again, and I reached out and hugged him. My life really was changing.

I never cried and hugged so much in my life. He held me tight and simply said, "Thank you."

I said, "Don't thank me, thank Jesus. He's already saved me and brought me joy. Let him do the same for you."

I couldn't believe how I was talking. If someone told me a few months earlier what I would be doing and the people I would be helping, I would have had them locked up for insanity. We went outside and talked for a while. I wrote down my phone number in case he needed someone to talk to, even though I made sure to let him know that Jesus was always there, ready to listen. Each service went well, and I couldn't believe I was standing in front of that many people, telling them the things that had happened in my life.

Each week after that, I would see that young couple at church. A couple of weeks went by when I didn't see them, and I started to feel concerned. The following week, they both returned, holding in their arms a small baby. I went up to them after service for an introduction of the new addition to their family. The young man pulled the blanket away from her face and said, "This is Sarah. Sarah, this is the man that helped save Daddy's life." God was able to use a man who had no desire to live to save someone else. Each week, I saw that proud father as he carried his child, a child he thought he would never see. He was a constant reminder that I could be used and, in God's eyes, I was something special.

I gave my testimony several years later at the church I was attending. Afterward, when I was in the lobby talking to people and handing out books, a young lady came up to me with tears in her eyes. All she could say was thank you, and you don't know what you've done for me. There were a lot of people there, and she asked for my email address so she could contact me. A couple of days later, I received this email from her:

Hi Mark,

This is Ashley from Calvary Chapel Oceanside. I spoke to you briefly on Sunday after the first service, and you said it would be okay to give you a call if I ever wanted to talk. Well, I want to talk. I want to share my story with you. But I decided to send you an email, mainly because I'm a much better writer than I am when I talk. But anyway, I guess I can date back the beginning of my depression to about 4 years ago when I was 19. I had just been to a gynecologist and given some pretty grim news. I followed the doctor's orders and found myself in the middle of a girl's medical nightmare. But during that time, I also began to date a guy who took very good care of me. I was pretty sure that this man was Mr. Right, the one I had been waiting for.

As my medical problems seemed to be getting worse, so was my relationship with my boyfriend. It was over. He said I had become too much to handle. *My mood swings, the dangerous things he caught me doing (I tried committing suicide by swallowing pills by this point two times, I think). When he broke up with me, I was sure that my life was over. The man that I had given everything to just left me. There was nothing left to live for. The years I have spent struggling with doctors, surgeries, and pain were all for nothing. Did I mention that there was nothing left to live for? So, without a second thought, I ran to my kitchen and found a bottle of rum, then ran to my bathroom and found a bottle of prescription painkillers. With both in my hand, I turned on the TV in my living room and gulped down both like I was snacking on Doritos and a Pepsi. I passed out... but hours later, I woke up.*

With a wicked hangover and an awful stomachache, I realized it didn't work. To be honest, I don't quite remember how it happened, what I said, or who I talked to, but I knew I needed help. I got myself to the emergency room and, from there, was put on a 3-day hold at the neuropsychological ward at UCI. I was given anti-depressants, diagnosed bipolar, released on that third day, and they said I was cured! As long as I took that medication, depression would never bother me again. But it did... my medical problems were only getting worse to the point where simple things like walking, tying my shoes, or getting in the car were excruciating pain. I COULDN'T TAKE IT ANYMORE! But then I met a new guy... (a guy who I tried dating but soon realized we should only be friends), and he told me about this really awesome place called church. I had attended church before and even liked it, but beyond my Sunday visits, that was it. So I started attending with him.

For Christmas, he bought me a beautiful study bible and told me I should read it! The thought of reading the bible had never crossed my mind up until that point... he even told me that he thought through God's strength, I might even be able to get off of my medication. So I did! He also told me that maybe I should pray for strength and joy and maybe even ask the Lord to give my medical team wisdom. I did these things... and it helped. I felt happier than I had in a while, but my physical pain was still worsening! And it was the Friday night before I met you this past Sunday that I told this friend that I didn't want to be a Christian anymore. My newfound passion for the Lord is over. I couldn't stand to love a God who watched me suffer. But he asked me to come to church on Sunday anyway. So I did it, not for me, not for Jesus, but for him. And then you came up on stage... and I cried. A lot. I had been entertaining the thought of a bottle of rum and a bottle of painkillers again. I had been thinking about getting back on my anti-depressants. But you know what?

I am pretty sure that God sent you up on that stage for me. I read your book last night. I circled words, underlined scripture, and highlighted sentences. I am so excited to be alive. Not because my life is going great. In fact, it's pretty bad right now. I am still sad, and I still have medical issues. But for the very first time ever, I have given ALL control of my life to the Lord. I read and re-read Jeremiah 29:11, and I actually feel joy! I am not sure what my life holds, where my 'diagnosis' will lead me, and the struggles I am going to face, but I quote a very wise man when I say that I will not cheat the world out of the gift God asks me to give. I now know the secret to getting over my depression... I will stop making it all about me. I am going to start making it all about God. I thank God for you. I thank God that you had to go through all of that because your testimony has given me mine. I know that being a true Christian is going to be an uphill battle, but as weak as I am... I'm ready. I would be lying if I said I am so much better, but for the first time, I see the light at the end of the tunnel, and that hope is enough for me to keep carrying on.

Thank you, Mark... I am now ready to get over depression.

My testimony started a change in her, and she wanted to let God guide her life. My advice to her was to find out what gifts, talents, and passions God has given her and use them for His glory. She told me she always had a heart for the junior high kids, and she was going back to her church further up north to volunteer her time. My wife and I kept in touch with her, and one day, she asked if she could come over and bring a friend. She had been seeing the leader of the junior high ministry and wanted us to meet him. They were married a year later, and God touched her body and diminished her pain. They adopted a baby a year after they were married; his name is John. I received a letter from her, she was going to Africa on a mission trip. If you go to her Facebook page, you can see she gives all the glory to her Lord. Ashley and her husband are licensed foster parents and even adopted a pregnant teenage girl, and now they are grandparents. She is an amazing woman and, with her husband, is accomplishing so much. What a testimony to be used for God's glory.

So, how does God want to use you? The only way to find out is to let Him.

"For it is God who works in you both to will and to do for His good pleasure."

— Philippians 2:13

Using what God has given you for His glory is living life to the full. There are so many people out in this world suffering and headed for the destination of hell. You might be their only hope, and no matter what the results might be, you honored God with your choice to use your gifts.

Chapter Six — Life Isn't Easy, But Worth It

My list can go on and on about how God used someone so worthless to make a difference to others. If you are still breathing, God isn't done with you. He has a plan for your life.

"'For I know the plans I have for you,' declares the LORD, 'plans to prosper you and not to harm you, plans to give you hope and a future."

— **Jeremiah 29:11**

See, He doesn't need to practice; He knows exactly what He is doing, even though we may not understand. His hand was there every time I tried to end my life, knowing He still had a use for me. We're not mass-produced, but each one of us is custom-made and made for a purpose. Our creator took great care and thought when He made you, as stated in the Psalms:

"For you created my inmost being; you knit me together in my mother's womb."

— **Psalm 139:13**

Life Isn't Easy, but Worth It

"I praise you because I am fearfully and wonderfully made; your works are wonderful, I know that full well."

— Psalm 139:14

"My frame was not hidden from you when I was made in the secret place. When I was woven together in the depths of the earth."

— Psalm 139:15

"Your eyes saw my unformed body. All the days ordained for me were written in your book before one of them came to be."

— Psalm 139:16

Will your life be easy once you become a follower of Christ? Jesus told us it won't:

"I have told you these things so that in me you may have peace. In this world, you will have trouble. But take heart! I have overcome the world."

— John 16:33

It would have been nice if Jesus said, "You might have some troubles, or there is a possibility of you having troubles," but no, He said we will have troubles, and He is right.

Getting Over Depression

A few years after being saved, I felt God calling me to go to Kentucky, and I knew it was God because I didn't want to go. I prayed with everyone, including each pastor at the church, to make sure this was God's will. My best friend, Mark, told me it didn't make sense since everything was going well here in California, and I thought great, let's pray. After we prayed, he looked at me and said, "I'm sure going to miss you, buddy." Our house sold in a day for more than we asked for, and my wife went ahead and found a new home in Kentucky. When I arrived in Kentucky, I felt called to go to a nursing home. There was one close by, and I went to the receptionist and asked if there was anyone who might want some company.

A heartbreaking statistic is that seventy percent of all people who go into a nursing home never receive a visitor. She directed me to a room where there were two lovely ladies, and I introduced myself. They started talking right away as if we had known each other for years. It was lunchtime, and I asked them what their favorite food was. And one said shrimp and the other fish, but they both agreed Long John Silver's had the best. There happened to be a Long John Silver's down the street, so I asked permission from the nurse to buy lunch for them. When I got back, we all had lunch, and I asked what they disliked about being at the nursing home, and they both said in unison that the food was terrible. When I got back home, God put on my heart that I was going to do a fancy dinner for the residents in a nursing home, and He even made it clear it was going to be about 120 people. It just so happened this nursing home had about 120 people staying there, so I thought this was a no-brainer. I made an appointment with the dietician, and she told me no, that they had to maintain certain dietary guidelines. I explained this was going to be a fancy dinner, but she still said no.

Time passed, and I was having a difficult time finding a job, and money was running out. I couldn't understand why God would have me move somewhere and not bless me for obeying. He put the same scripture on my heart that I put on the card I gave to the homeless.

"Trust in the LORD with all your heart and lean not on your own understanding."

— Proverbs 3:5

"In all your ways, acknowledge him, and he will make your paths straight."

— Proverbs 3:6

I couldn't miss it; it seemed to be everywhere. There was even one Sunday during service when the pastor asked if anyone needed prayer to come up. My heart had been so troubled that I went up immediately. As the pastor was praying, he said God had put on his heart Proverbs 3:5 and 6, and before he could say it, I quoted the scripture and then fell on my knees and wept out loud.

I finally found a job as the assistant catering manager for the University of Kentucky, a job I was well overqualified for, but at least it was something. I wasn't making enough to pay the bills, so I was slowly going further and further in debt, borrowing money from life insurance policies and running up credit card debt. I was falling back into depression, more focused on my problems than why God had me there. Occasionally, I would remember about the dinner for the nursing home and visit one from time to time with no luck.

One day, several months later, someone told me about this small nursing home with only 50 residents, and I thought to myself, that can't be it, but I made an appointment with the home manager. I talked to her and told her about my vision for this dinner. I described the menu of braised beef tenderloin, roasted garlic potatoes, fresh green beans, and homemade desserts. She was so excited and began to cry. She explained that she wanted to make a dinner where the residents could invite guests, and she told me it would be for about 120 people altogether. I almost fell out of my chair when she told me the number. I started my quest in April, and now it's November, getting close to Christmas.

I had no money for food and approached the pastor of our church. The pastor had me go before the church and explain the vision, and the people were excited. People donated more than enough money, talent, and precious time. The University allowed me to borrow all the equipment and dinnerware I would need. It was just a couple of weeks before Christmas, and the ladies from the church converted a plain cinder block walled room into a festive and beautiful dining room. They brought gifts for each resident and centerpieces that would take your breath away. I had my church family dress up in black pants, a white shirt, ties, and a black apron; even our pastor was a waiter for the night.

The room was filled with the residents and their guests, and everyone was treated as royalty, as if Jesus himself was there (and He was). The food came out perfectly and served hot to each guest. Another statistic is that ninety percent of all residents of a nursing home live less than a year. So, this would be the last Christmas for most that attended that night, but what a night. Unfortunately, I wasn't enjoying this magnificent evening as much as everyone else because I was slipping back into depression, focused on my problems instead of what God was trying to show me. After serving all the meals, one of the ladies from our church came up to me crying, saying, "I did it, I did it." I asked what she did, and she told me she witnessed someone and that they received Jesus as Lord and Savior. You see, some of the guests couldn't make it to the table that night; they were restricted to their beds, so some of the meals were served in their rooms.

The lady who was restricted to her bed asked why they were doing this, and her server explained about the love of God and how they wanted others to see His love through them. In front of her family, who was in the room with her, she received the greatest gift ever. The next day was Sunday, and our pastor told the congregation that the nursing home manager called and told him that the woman who was saved that night went home to the Lord at 2 am.

A couple of months went by, and my job at the university was eliminated, so I was out of work again. We were in dire straits with the mortgage coming due and nowhere else to borrow. I was in my room crying and shouting at God, "Why is this happening to me?" I did what you told me to do, and everything is going wrong. As I was lying on the floor feeling sorry for myself, it was as if God reached down and grabbed me and said, "I thought you wanted to do my will. If I wanted you to go to Kentucky to bring one of my children home to me, why aren't you honored?" I never felt so ashamed. I was so busy looking at me that I couldn't see Him and what He was doing through me. A couple of days later, I received a phone call from a company in California I used to work for. They wanted to hire me as a consultant and would fly me out. My first week's paycheck would be enough to pay my house payment and a couple of other bills that needed to be paid. Even though I forgot about God, He never forgot about me.

After completing the week, I was asked to stay on, and the amount that was offered was very generous. I went back to Kentucky and explained the offer, and felt it was time for us to go back to California. My wife agreed that I needed to take the job, but she wasn't ready to move back to California. I made arrangements to stay with a friend in California temporarily until things got resolved and I started my new job. I had the company mail the check to my wife so she could take care of our bills. Three months went by, and I called my wife. I told her she belongs with me and should come back to California. She still wasn't ready to move. I explained I couldn't stay with my friend any longer. It was just too big of an imposition for him, and I needed to find a place to live. I drove back to Kentucky to get the rest of my things, and we agreed that she would send me all the bills, and I would take care of them and send her money for the mortgage. We agreed to trust God in our marriage and to give it up to Him.

I moved into a small one-bedroom apartment near the ocean. Every morning, I would get up at two AM, walk along the beach, and pray before I went to work. Eight months went by, and I was having our taxes done. Since I took my wages as an I-9 without having taxes taken out, we owed a few thousand dollars. As I told my wife, she told me she had another I-9 form. I asked her what it was for, and she told me when her mother passed away, she received several thousand dollars from an insurance policy. I told her I needed help paying our taxes, and she could either send me some of the money or I would have to stop sending money for the mortgage. She told me she wasn't going to send me any money and in two weeks I received a letter from a lawyer. The letter stated that my wife was filing for a divorce, and she wanted everything except the bills. I was in shock and didn't know what to do, so I got on my knees immediately and asked God for direction.

After I calmed down, I called my wife of over thirty-two years and asked what was going on. She told me she had no desire to move back to California and that her mother left her some money, and she was going to buy the house on her own. I told her I read the letter and to make sure I was reading it right, I asked if she was asking me to give up everything we owned and for me to pay all the bills, and she wanted to keep the life insurance policy while I still paid for it. She told me that is what she was asking, plus four hundred dollars a month. I told her I would have to get back to her. I continued to pray about what I should do, and God put it on my heart.

"If anyone does not provide for his relatives, and especially for his immediate family, he has denied the faith and is worse than an unbeliever."

— 1 Timothy 5:8

I called her back and told her I would agree to everything except the four hundred dollars a month so that she could have all the possessions, and I would take the liability of paying all the debt. Still, I didn't feel it was right that I should continue to give her money, and she agreed immediately. I then told her I thought what she was doing was wrong and that we should not be getting this divorce; no matter what, I would be there for her. She then told me she did need something from me, and I asked her what it was. She told me they needed to fax the title of the house as soon as the divorce was final so she could keep the interest rate on the loan she acquired. It took only two weeks before the divorce was final. I remember the day before the hearing in Kentucky when my wife called me. I again told her she shouldn't be doing this and that God hated divorce, but all she could say was where do you want the papers faxed to?

All I could think was okay, God, now what am I supposed to be doing? Have you ever been there? You think you're doing what is right, you're serving in the church, being a good example at work, praying, and studying your Bible, yet life is not going the way you feel it should. It should be easier, right? Where's the blessings Lord? I remember every morning, I still got up at 2 in the morning to pray, and as I walked, I got to a particular place and asked God just to take me. Bring me home, Lord. I would cry, but I added something new to my plea. I said not my will, but yours be done. My problem was that I was looking at my life through my eyes, not God's.

As time went by, I was at church doing the food ministry on Saturday night. A woman who worked in the ministry asked me how I was doing, and I explained I was having a rough time. I knew this lady from volunteering at the church but never knew her name. Teri was her name, and she was one of those people who loved to serve but was always in the background, serving with a humble heart. Teri said if I ever needed someone to talk to or share a meal, she would be available. I took her up on her offer, and we had breakfast one Sunday morning. It was a wonderful time as Teri listened patiently and told me a little about herself. I asked if we could do this again, and she consented. There was something special about Teri; it was wonderful just to be with her. She would share about her life and her love for God. She had so much more faith than I did. She became my best friend, someone I could talk to openly about how I was feeling and what I was going through. To make a long story short, after a year, we were married at the church we served in. I could never love anyone the way I love Teri.

I look forward to seeing her each day, and there is something so special about serving together. God has given me this unbelievable blessing to remind me of His love for me. So now, when Satan knocks at my door and tries to enter my thoughts, all I need to do is think of Teri because she reminds me of God's love.

I would like to tell you that was the last trial I had to endure, but I'm afraid I'll be going through them until I get home. Only a few months after the marriage, I got very sick and wasn't sure I was going to make it; we had to put Teri's dog to sleep, the company I was working at sold, and I was out of a job, and we lost our home.

However, I have never gone back to the deep pit of depression. The difference now is my focus is on my maker. When the enemy pulls me toward the pit, God is pulling me toward His grace. You see, now I have the memories of the people who were touched because God allows this life to go on, and I want to see what else He has in store for me. You only throw away what is worthless, and once you see the value, you treasure it. Allow God to open your eyes to the treasure He has put into your life so that you may treasure it almost as much as God does. There is a saying, "God can't guide your steps until you move your feet." He has so many blessings for us, but He is not a DoorDash God. He doesn't deliver while you are sitting at home; you must get up and pick up the blessings. That's right; blessings are so numerous that it would be hard to count. Unfortunately,

God will not force us on the path; He will, however, guide us if we let Him.

Chapter Seven —
Adversity

I had someone ask me if I felt depression was real or something we make up in our minds. I told her I believed it was a real infirmity and that I still suffered from it. I believe there are two types of depression; one is circumstantial. That is when something drastic happens in your life, like the loss of a loved one, a financial disaster, an accident, or a major illness. Circumstantial depression would typically go away over time as the situation mends, but clinical depression is something that you most likely will be battling for the rest of your life. Paul said:

"And lest I should be exalted above measure by the abundance of the revelations, a thorn in the flesh was given to me, a messenger of Satan to buffet me, lest I be exalted above measure, 8 Concerning this thing, I pleaded with the Lord three times that it might depart from me."

— 2 Corinthians 12:7-10

God has given us different gifts and abilities. I also believe we have our own thorns that we are called to deal with. Thorns can be medical conditions, where we were raised, conditions surrounding our childhood, disabilities, or depression. These thorns are painful, but we have a choice to focus on the thorn or the one who can relieve our pain. Satan is hoping the pain will be too overwhelming for us to seek any comfort and reside in ourselves to just suffer the pain. However, if we turn to Jesus and make Him the focus of our lives, admit we can't do it without Him, and humbly submit to His will, our lives will take on a whole other meaning. Paul continued to say,

"And He said to me, 'My grace is sufficient for you, for My strength is made perfect in weakness.' Therefore, most gladly, I will rather boast in my infirmities that the power of Christ may rest upon me. Therefore, I take pleasure in infirmities, in reproaches, in needs, in persecutions, in distresses, for Christ's sake. For when I am weak, then I am strong."

— 2 Corinthians 12:9-10

Let us never forget that this is not our home; we have an eternal home where there will no longer be any more thorns.

"And God will wipe away every tear from their eyes; there shall be no more death, nor sorrow, nor crying. There shall be no more pain, for the former things have passed away. Then He

who sat on the throne said, 'Behold, I make all things new.' And He said to me, 'Write, for these words are true and faithful.'"

— Revelations 21:4-5

For now, we are called to live the best life that we can, helping people God has surrounded us with, and He has given us the tools to do that. We have an opportunity to turn that thorn into a sword to defeat the enemy that has so many held captive. People will listen to people who are dealing with the same thorn as they have, and if you are living your life with our Lord, others will take notice and will seek the comfort God has given you. Be a light to others and show them how to get relief from their pain.

I was reading an article about Robin Williams's suicide. The article was written by his wife, Susan, and it was entitled, "The terrorist inside my husband's brain." I thought, what a great description of depression. What does a terrorist do? He comes to steal, kill, and to destroy. A well-prepared terrorist would know when to attack, where his enemy is most vulnerable, where he could do the most damage, and would be equipped to attack. The terrorist in our brain is Satan, and he is the best at what he does. Unfortunately, we stand no chance alone against him in this fight. Satan is the ruler of this world, and even Jesus told us that. Each day, we are in the fight of our lives, and we can't win it alone. Without God, we are already defeated. Satan rules this world, but he doesn't have to rule you.

"Jesus answered and said, 'This voice did not come because of Me but for your sake.' Now is the judgment of this world; now, the ruler of this world will be cast out. And I, if I am lifted up from the earth, will draw all peoples to Myself."

— John 12:30-32

Benefits of Adversity

We are so busy feeling bad over adversity that we don't see any benefit that might come from it, but there are a few:

1. Prevents Pride in My Life

"But He gives more grace. Therefore, He says: 'God resists the proud, but gives grace to the humble.'"

— James 4:6

2. Increases Dependence on God

"The LORD is my rock, my fortress, and my deliverer; my God is my rock, in whom I take refuge. He is my shield and the horn of my salvation, my stronghold."

— Psalm 18:2

3. Keeps Who I am in Perspective. You Belong to God

"But you are a chosen people, a royal priesthood, a holy nation, a people belonging to God, that you may declare the praises of him who called you out of darkness into his wonderful light."

— 1 Peter 2:9

4. Strengthens and Deepens My Faith

"I tell you the truth, anyone who has faith in me will do what I have been doing. He will do even greater things than these because I am going to the Father."

— John 14:12

5. Prepares Me for Greater Service

"For we are God's workmanship, created in Christ Jesus to do good works, which God prepared in advance for us to do."

— Ephesians 2:10

6. Count it All Joy

"My brethren, count it all joy when you fall into various trials."

— James 1:2

You have to be kidding. How can we call it all joy when we go through the trials of this world? The apostles must not have realized what we were going to be going through, or they would have thought twice about this verse. Financial hardships, health problems, family difficulties, the loss of loved ones, work issues, and the list goes on. Okay, the apostle Paul might have been able to sympathize with us.

"From the Jews five times, I received forty stripes minus one. Three times I was beaten with rods; once I was stoned; three times I was shipwrecked; a night and a day I have been in the deep; in journeys often, in perils of waters, in perils of robbers, in perils of my own countrymen, in perils of the Gentiles, in perils in the city, in perils in the wilderness, in perils in the sea, in perils among false brethren; in weariness and toil, in sleeplessness often, in hunger and thirst, in fasting often, in cold and nakedness."

— 2 Corinthians 11:24-27

And he was still able to say:

"And not only that, but we also glory in tribulations, knowing that tribulation produces perseverance."

— Romans 5:3

"And perseverance, character; and character, hope."

— Romans 5:4

But the other disciples, how hard did they have it?

"Beloved, do not think it strange concerning the fiery trial which is to try you, as though some strange thing happened to you; but rejoice to the extent that you partake of Christ's sufferings, that when His glory is revealed, you may also be glad with exceeding joy."

— 1 Peter 4:12-13

Oh yes, they were all persecuted and tortured and put to death, except for John, who was only boiled in oil and then exiled to an island for the rest of his life. Okay, they knew what real trials and tribulations were, so how did they do it? How could they still rejoice during it, and why can't I? Jesus said:

"Blessed are you when they revile and persecute you and say all kinds of evil against you falsely for My sake. Rejoice and be exceedingly glad, for great is your reward in heaven, for so they persecuted the prophets who were before you."

— Matthew 5:11-12

That's my problem. I'm so focused on the trial, and in this life, I can't see the reward. I remember when Teri and I were going to Hawaii on vacation. The weeks before seemed easier at work because my focus was on my vacation and the fun I was planning on having. As

Christians, we are all going to be going on the best vacation ever, and it will never end. When I was going to Hawaii, I looked up where we were going and found out as much as I could about it. What we could do, eat, what we wanted to see, so we would be prepared and excited about our trip. That is what I'm doing now, trying to find out as much as I can about my eternal vacation. I look through my brochure, the bible, and other books to get me excited about my trip, and that puts this life in perspective.

I'm here to glorify God, and in return, I earn rewards that I can use in Heaven. I believe that is how the apostles looked at this life as an opportunity to turn their pain into gifts for the Lord. Imagine when others saw them still rejoicing when they were enduring so much for the Lord; that's what spread Christianity. That's the same with us today; if others can see us rejoicing through the suffering we might be going through, it will change them. They are going to want to know where our joy comes from, and that is our opportunity to point them in the direction of Jesus. The only thing we can bring to Heaven is people. May we be focused on the best time we are ever going to have and bring as many as we can...

"Set your mind on things above, not on things on the earth."

— **Colossians 3:2**

Chapter Eight — What Can Cause Depression?

Can a faithful and growing believer get depressed? According to a recent poll, one out of every five people suffer from depression; I'm not talking about the times when someone might feel a little down, but severe depression, to the point where people need to seek the guidance of counselors and medication. That doesn't mean the other four were Christians. The definition found in the dictionary for depression: A state of general emotional dejection, despair, sadness, hopelessness, and sometimes suicidal tendencies.

"The troubles of my heart have multiplied; free me from my anguish."

— PS 25:17

Satan has numerous weapons he uses: lies, deceit, greed, desperation, feelings of self-doubt, hopelessness, and rejection. I think he uses these fiery darts to aim at a target, and the bull's eye is depressed. If Satan hits that bull's eye, it can lead to separation from God, hopelessness, the desire for death, and, in extreme cases, suicide. So, do

What Can Cause Depression?

Christians suffer from depression? The Bible gives us some examples of people who had reached a point in their lives where they would have preferred being dead or wished they had never been born. When we look at the lives of some of these righteous men, we can identify several factors that lead to depression. We also discover several ways in which God calls us to respond to it.

One of the great men of faith was Elijah. His cause of depression was *fear* of what might happen to him. Shortly after, Elijah challenged the prophets of Baal to have their god bring fire down to burn their sacrifices. All day, the prophets of Baal called on their god to no avail. Elijah, at that time, was full of confidence and not worried, knowing everything was going according to God's plan.

"At noon, Elijah began to taunt them. 'Shout louder!' he said. 'Surely he is a god! Perhaps he is deep in thought, or busy, or traveling. Maybe he is sleeping and must be awakened.' So they shouted louder and slashed themselves with swords and spears, as was their custom, until their blood flowed. Midday passed, and they continued their frantic prophesying until it was time for the evening sacrifice. But there was no response, no one answered, no one paid attention."

— 1 King 18:27-29

Now, things are going his way. The priests had failed, and now it was Elijah's turn; he poured water all over his sacrifice and called on the One and only True and Living God.

"At the time of sacrifice, the prophet Elijah stepped forward and prayed: 'O LORD, God of Abraham, Isaac, and Israel, let it be known today that you are God in Israel and that I am your servant and have done all these things at your command. Answer me, O LORD, answer me, so these people will know that you, O LORD, are God and that you are turning their hearts back again.'"

— 1 King 18:36-37

The Lord brought fire down to burn the sacrifices. Elijah put to death 450 prophets of Baal. How does a person go from seeing one of God's great miracles and then falls into a deep depression, so deep that he no longer wants to live?

"Now Ahab told Jezebel everything Elijah had done and how he had killed all the prophets with the sword. So Jezebel sent a messenger to Elijah to say, 'May the gods deal with me, be it ever so severely, if by this time tomorrow, I do not make your life like that of one of them.'"

— 1 King 19:1-2

What Can Cause Depression?

"Elijah was afraid and ran for his life. When he came to Beersheba in Judah, he left his servant there while he himself went on a day's journey into the desert. He came to a broom tree, sat down under it, and prayed that he might die. 'I have had enough, LORD,' he said. 'Take my life; I am no better than my ancestors.' Then he lay down under the tree and fell asleep."

— 1 King 19:3-5

Fear is a powerful force in our lives, and we would rather do anything other than face it, even wish we were dead. There is an acronym for Fear of False Evidence Appearing Real. Nothing happened to Elijah; it was only a threat from someone he must have felt was more powerful than God. Elijah must not have thought it out. God just used him in an unbelievably powerful way, killing four hundred and fifty men, and now he is afraid of a threat from one woman.

Think about the things God has delivered you from. Have you ever felt like you have had enough, and you don't think you can take it anymore? You become afraid, you are full of hopelessness, and you don't want to see another day; you just don't know how you can possibly make it through? Place this verse in your heart:

"For I am the LORD, your God, who takes hold of your right hand and says to you, Do not fear; I will help you."

— **Isaiah 41:13**

Another major cause of depression is *loss*. Loss of a loved one, health, finances, and anything else we hold dear to us. Job was a God-loving man who lived a righteous life, and in just one day, he lost everything he had. He was sitting at the table, and messengers kept coming in telling him that he had lost his donkeys and oxen, and then he had lost his sheep and servants, next his camels, and finally his sons and daughters. He still held strong in his faith and trusted in the Lord, then his body became inflicted with terrible sores, and he lost his health.

"So Satan went out from the presence of the LORD and afflicted Job with painful sores from the soles of his feet to the top of his head. [8] Then Job took a piece of broken pottery and scraped himself with it as he sat among the ashes."

— **Job 2:7-8**

Then we get to the point of self-pity, and much too often, we point the finger of blame at others or God as Job did while talking to God; he says:

What Can Cause Depression?

"Why then did you bring me out of the womb? I wish I had died before any eye saw me."

— Job 10:18

"If only I had never come into being or had been carried straight from the womb to the grave!"

— Job 10:19

"Are not my few days almost over? Turn away from me so I can have a moment's joy."

— Job 10:20

"Before I go to the place of no return, to the land of gloom and deep shadow."

— Job 10:21

"To the land of deepest night, of deep shadow and disorder, where even the light is like darkness."

— Job 10:22

So, instead of trusting God, we blame Him. Have you ever said, "I wish I was never born?" Life is just so terrible that you wish you never existed. It's amazing how we can feel so bad at one moment that we are able to disregard an entire lifetime of blessings.

"Blessed be the God and Father of our Lord Jesus Christ, who has blessed us with every spiritual blessing in the heavenly places in Christ."

— Ephesians 1:3

Sometimes, we get depressed simply because things aren't going the way we want them to. Have you ever gotten so mad and depressed because things *don't go your way?* You feel as if God doesn't care, so why should you? Maybe someone you hate is doing good, and it drives you crazy. I know, in my life, some of my best moments were times when someone else was doing worse than me, and in turn, some of my worst moments were when someone was doing better. A friend of mine recently got a divorce, and when I saw him, he was down. I asked him what was troubling him. He explained how well his wife and children seemed to be doing without him, and that drove him into depression. Look at Jonah's words.

"He prayed to the LORD, 'LORD, is this not what I said when I was still at home? That is why I was so quick to flee to Tarshish. I knew that you are a gracious and compassionate God, slow to anger and abounding in love, a God who relents from sending calamity. Now, O LORD, take away my life, for it is better for me to die than to live.'"

What Can Cause Depression?

Jonah was just saved from certain death by being swallowed by a large fish, but instead of being thankful for his good fortune, he was depressed because the people he hated were doing well. He didn't get his way.

"As the heavens are higher than the earth, so are my ways higher than your ways and my thoughts than your thoughts."

— Isaiah 55:9

Then there was Moses, a friend of God. Wow, what a title. Here is a man who talked to God and saw all the miracles God worked through him, and yet his faith and strength are no greater than ours at times. We all come to a point where we are *overwhelmed* because we are so focused on what we can only do instead of what God can do through us.

"He asked the LORD, 'Why have you brought this trouble on your servant? What have I done to displease you that you put the burden of all these people on me? Did I conceive all these people? Did I give them birth? Why do you tell me to carry them in my arms, as a nurse carries an infant, to the land you promised on oath to their forefathers? Where can I get meat for all these people? They keep wailing to me, 'Give us meat to eat!' I cannot carry all these people by myself; the burden is too heavy

for me. If this is how you are going to treat me, put me to death right now — if I have found favor in your eyes — and do not let me face my own ruin.'"

— Numbers 11:11-15

I felt as if I was always overwhelmed and carrying the weight of the world on my shoulders and that I could never catch a break. There was never enough time in the day, and if I didn't do it, it wasn't going to get done. Does any of this sound familiar to you? Do you live your day knowing you can't possibly get through it? Are you so overwhelmed with the thoughts in your head that you can't seem to get anything done? Believe me, you are not alone.

"Humble yourselves, therefore, under God's mighty hand, that he may lift you up in due time. Cast all your anxiety on him because he cares for you."

— 1 Peter 5:6-7

These were not mere men but the saints of the Bible. Men who spoke directly to God, and yet they were not free from feeling the full force of depression, the desire not to live.

I think that's what happened to Elijah, Moses, Jonah, and Job. Their lives were great when their focus was kept on the Lord and all the wonderful things He can do. When they put their focus on themselves without considering God's plan, feelings of hopelessness and depression come over them. They forgot about what God could do and focused on their own limited abilities, and they knew their abilities couldn't get them out of their mess.

God answers us all differently when we call on Him. When He finally answered Job, He was stern, to say the least, and let Job have it. He told Job, how dare you question God's motives and plans for your life.

"Will the one who contends with the Almighty correct him? Let him who accuses God answer him!"

— Job 40:2

Even though God was stern with Job, He gave him a chance to repent. He restored Job's life and made him prosperous. God gave him twice as much as he had before and even blessed him with seven sons and three daughters.

"Now the LORD blessed the latter days of Job more than his beginning, for he had fourteen thousand sheep, six thousand camels, one thousand yoke of oxen, and one thousand female donkeys. He also had seven sons and three daughters."

— Job 42:12-13

For Elijah, God sent an angel to restore and comfort him.

"Then he lay down under the tree and fell asleep. All at once, an angel touched him and said, 'Get up and eat.' He looked around, and there by his head was a cake of bread baked over hot coals and a jar of water. He ate and drank and then lay down again."

— 1 Kings 19:5-6

The angel fed him and gave him rest so God could help him get his mind back on the right track. I believe that during that time, Elijah remembered all the great things the Lord had done and realized that there was nothing He couldn't do. Elijah had been able to restore his body and his mind and rebuild his faith, so he was better equipped to move on.

What about Jonah? I think God should have laid him out for his disobedience. Even when he finally did what God called him to do, he did it in a halfhearted way. Yet God knows what each one of us needs, and He took the time to show Jonah why He did what he did for Nineveh, even though he is God and doesn't owe us any explanation.

"Jonah went out and sat down at a place east of the city. There, he made himself a shelter, sat in its shade, and waited to see what would happen to the city. Then the LORD God provided a

vine and made it grow up over Jonah to give shade for his head
to ease his discomfort, and Jonah was very happy about the
vine. But at dawn the next day, God provided a worm, which
chewed the vine so that it withered. When the sun rose, God
provided a scorching east wind, and the sun blazed on Jonah's
head so that he grew faint. He wanted to die and said, 'It would
be better for me to die than to live.'"

— Jonah 4:5-8

"*But God said to Jonah, 'Do you have a right to be angry about*
the vine?' 'I do,' he said. 'I am angry enough to die.'"

— Jonah 4:9

"*But the LORD said, 'You have been concerned about this vine,*
though you did not tend it or make it grow. It sprang up
overnight and died overnight. But Nineveh has more than a
hundred and twenty thousand people who cannot tell their right
hand from their left, and many cattle as well. Should I not be
concerned about that great city?'"

— Jonah 4:10

Then, there was Moses. God proved repeatedly that there was nothing He couldn't do, but God's love for us is never-ending.

"The LORD said to Moses: "Bring me seventy of Israel's elders who are known to you as leaders and officials among the people. Have them come to the Tent of the Meeting so that they may stand there with you. I will come down and speak with you there, and I will take of the Spirit that is on you and put the Spirit on them. They will help you carry the burden of the people so that you will not have to carry it alone."

— Numbers 11:16-17

"Tell the people: Consecrate yourselves in preparation for tomorrow, when you will eat meat. The LORD heard you when you wailed, 'If only we had meat to eat! We were better off in Egypt!' Now the LORD will give you meat, and you will eat it. You will not eat it for just one day, or two days, or five, ten, or twenty days, but for a whole month — until it comes out of your nostrils and you loathe it — because you have rejected the LORD, who is among you, and have wailed before him, saying, 'Why did we ever leave Egypt?'"

— Numbers 11:18-20

"But Moses said, 'Here I am among six hundred thousand men on foot, and you say, 'I will give them meat to eat for a whole month!' Would they have enough if flocks and herds were slaughtered for them? Would they have enough if all the fish in the sea were caught for them?'"

What Can Cause Depression?

— **Numbers 11:21-22**

"The LORD answered Moses, 'Is the LORD's arm too short? You will now see whether or not what I say will come true for you.'"

— **Numbers 11:23**

He explained to Moses what to do, and then God gave them their request for meat. Why would God care so much for people who seem unappreciative, self-centered, and worthless at times? Because He loves us. We'll probably never understand why, but He does.

Chapter Nine — Just as God Intended

Have you ever wondered why you're here or if there is any purpose for your existence? Do you ever feel like I did, that God made a mistake, and the world would be better off without you? If you ever felt that way, you need to see yourself through the eyes of God. Just think, the creator of all designed you exactly the way you are. He didn't need the practice; He knows exactly what He is doing, and He makes no mistakes.

"Before I formed you in the womb, I knew you; Before you were born, I sanctified you; I ordained you a prophet to the nations."

— Jeremiah 1:5

There is a purpose for our existence and a reason you are exactly the way you are. God has a plan for you. You need to see yourself through God's eyes and ask Him What He desires of you. You can't pound a nail in with a can opener or open a can with a hammer. Each tool is designed for a specific purpose. It is the same with us. Unless we are doing what we are created to do, we are not going to be much use to ourselves, others, or God, but when we discover our purpose, the world will open up to us.

God has given each of us gifts and talents to be used in a specific way for a reason. We have been created to make a difference and an impact in this world, and each one of us has a unique role, which only we can fill as God intended.

"We have different gifts, according to the grace given us. If a man's gift is prophesying, let him use it in proportion to his faith. If it is serving, let him serve; if it is teaching, let him teach; if it is encouraging, let him encourage; if it is contributing to the needs of others, let him give generously; if it is leadership, let him govern diligently; if it is showing mercy, let him do it cheerfully."

— Romans 12:6-8

Depression is the focus of negative feelings like uselessness, hopelessness, confusion, anger, sadness, hatred, and other useless emotions. However, when we are busy living our lives the way God has intended, we don't have the time to be depressed.

God sees something we don't see in ourselves. He sees someone He can love, use, and care for. He sees someone who can make a difference in this world, and if you spend time with Him, He'll show you that person. God makes no exceptions.

At a fund-raising dinner for a school that serves learning-disabled children, the father of one of the school's students delivered a speech that would never be forgotten by all who attended.

After extolling the school and its dedicated staff, he offered a question. "Everything God does is done with perfection. Yet, my son, Shay, cannot learn things as other children do. He cannot understand things as other children do. Where is God's plan reflected in my son?"

The audience was stilled by the query. The father continued, "I believe," the father answered, "that when God brings a childlike Shay into the world, an opportunity to realize the Divine Plan presents itself. And it comes in the way people treat that child." Then, he told this story:

Shay and I walked past a park where some boys Shay knew were playing baseball. Shay asked, "Do you think they will let me play?" I knew that most boys would not want him on their team. But I understood that if my son could play, it would give him a much-needed sense of belonging. I approached one of the boys on the field and asked if Shay could play. The boy looked around for guidance from his teammates. Getting none, he took matters into his own hands and said, "We are losing by six runs, and the game is in the eighth inning. I guess he can be on our team, and we'll try to put him up to bat in the ninth inning."

In the bottom of the eighth inning, Shay's team scored a few runs but was still behind by three. At the top of the ninth inning, Shay put on a glove and played in the outfield. Although no hits came his way, he was obviously ecstatic just to be on the field, grinning from ear to ear as I waved to him from the stands.

In the bottom of the ninth inning, Shay's team scored again. Now, with two outs and bases loaded, the potential winning run was on base. Shay was scheduled to be the next at-bat. Would the team let Shay bat at this juncture and give away their chance to win the game? Surprisingly, Shay was given the bat. Everyone knew that a hit was all but impossible because Shay didn't even know how to hold a bat properly, much less connect with the ball. However, as Shay stepped up to the plate, the pitcher moved up a few steps to lob the ball softly so Shay could at least make contact. The first pitch came, and Shay swung clumsily and missed. The pitcher again took a few steps forward to toss the ball softly toward Shay.

As the pitch came in, Shay swung at the ball and hit a slow ground ball to the pitcher. The pitcher picked up the soft grounder and could easily have thrown the ball to the first baseman. Shay would have been out, and that would have ended the game. Instead, the pitcher took the ball and threw it on a high arc to right field, far beyond the reach of the first baseman. Everyone started yelling, "Shay, run to first. Run to first." Never in his life had Shay ever made it to first base. He scampered down the baseline, wide-eyed and startled. Everyone yelled, "Run to second, run to second!"

By the time Shay was rounding first base, the right fielder had the ball. He could have thrown the ball to the second baseman for a tag. But the right fielder understood what the pitcher's intentions had been, so he threw the ball high and far over the third baseman's head. Shay ran toward second base as the runners ahead of him deliriously circled the bases toward home. As Shay reached second base, the opposing shortstop ran to him, turned him in the direction of third base, and shouted, "Run to third!" As Shay rounded third, the boys from both teams were screaming, "Shay! Run home!" Shay ran home, stepped on home plate, and was cheered as the hero for hitting a "grand slam" and winning the game for his team.

"That day," the boys from both teams helped bring a piece of the Divine Plan for my son into this world.

Don't cheat the world out of the gift God asks you to give.

"Remembering the words the Lord Jesus himself said: 'It is more blessed to give than to receive.'"

— Acts 20:35

Our Choices Affect Others

A while ago, a dear brother in Christ, Butch, was in a terrible car accident. A woman decided to drive the wrong way on the freeway and hit him head-on. Butch was in the hospital for five months and suffered multiple injuries; he now has more metal in his body than a Smart Car. Not only Butch but his wife Sammie went through pain that is almost unimaginable, along with family and friends. A choice caused this terrible event to happen. The lady, for some reason, chose to drive the wrong way on the road early that morning, and her choice didn't affect only her life but the lives of others. Isn't that what we see on the news?

Someone chooses to bring a gun to a nightclub to kill others or a movie theater, a suicide bomber chooses to strap a bomb and walk into a crowd of people, or a drunk driver decides to get in their car. Our choices affect so many other people. My life is made up of poor choices that changed the lives of those around me. Attempted suicide six different times, was admitted to mental hospitals, had poor financial choices, uncontrolled anger, and cared more about my needs than my family's. I changed people's lives for the worse most of my life. Once, when my daughter was a teenager, her boyfriend broke up with her, and she was devastated, so she took a bottle of aspirin and pills to take her life, and only through the grace of God did she survive.

Why would she take such drastic actions for something so insignificant because that is how her dad handled his problems? Our choices don't only define who we are but change those close to us. The biggest choice we'll ever make is whether we will receive Jesus as our Lord and Savior and allow him to guide us through this life until He brings us home, but it doesn't stop there. God gives us choices to make every day, and He wants to be part of each one. Our lives can bring death and despair to others, or they can encourage and save lives by the choices we make. Do we put someone down, or do we share Christ's love with them? Do we ignore someone in pain, or do we show them love and concern? Do we take part in this world or obey God? Do we give in to the lust in our hearts or pray for strength to glorify God?

There are so many choices, and to make the right one, we need to get the advice of our heavenly Father, who never makes mistakes. Choose the Lord; you'll never go wrong. Butch had choices to make. Does he wallow in his pain or use it for God's glory? He chose the latter; he and his wife praised God and trusted Him through this whole process. Facebook posts showed their faith in God to get Butch through this, and it did. The choice to post these amazing words throughout this ordeal was inspirational to so many and brought others closer to God. I know it did for me. Thank you, Butch and Sammie, for choosing Christ over adversity.

Chapter Ten — How to Conquer Depression

The definition of Insanity is doing the same thing over and over and expecting a different result.

Starting today, you need to start doing something different. You don't have to change your life or the way you have been doing everything, but change something. Read your Bible more, read Christian books, start a journal, read a daily devotional, memorize scripture that will help you when you get in trouble, serve others, join a home fellowship, find someone to hold you accountable, or pray more and let God lead you.

There is a great quote by Albert Einstein, "There are two ways to look at life, one as if there are no miracles, and the other as if everything is a miracle." Choose the latter.

Each day, I read the Bible to gain a better understanding of what it is God wants me to do. It's amazing how relevant the Bible is after thousands of years. I found answers to each of my questions and explanations of how I could combat and conquer depression in my life. These are some of the lessons I've learned through the word of God.

Take The Focus Off Myself

My life changed when I focused on the One who created me instead of on myself. Each day, I used to think of all the things I didn't have, all the things I wanted to have, the way I thought I should feel, why I wasn't like someone else, or just daydreaming of the person I wanted to be. Because of that focus, when I compared myself to others, I had feelings of insecurity, pride or inferiority, anger, hopelessness, confusion, and the list went on. Someone asked Jesus

"'Teacher, which is the greatest commandment in the Law?' or what is the most important thing we should do? Jesus replied: 'Love the Lord your God with all your heart and with all your

soul and with all your mind.' This is the first and greatest commandment. And the second is like it: 'Love your neighbor as yourself.'"

— Matthew 22:36-39

God is telling us not to live our lives with the focus on ourselves but on Him and the wellbeing of others.

"Do nothing out of selfish ambition or vain conceit, but in humility consider others better than yourselves. Each of you should look not only to your own interests but also to the interests of others."

— Philippians 2:3-4

I learned that if I focused on God and others, God's focus was on me, and I was no longer a slave of my destructive thoughts.

My sister, Kathy, is one of the best examples of putting others before herself. She treats everyone the same, with love and respect, and she enjoys the fruit of her love.

I remember going to a restaurant with her, and sitting across from us was an elderly couple, just slowly eating their meal. Both of them were eating but didn't seem to be aware of each other's presence. They seemed totally oblivious to their surroundings and even appeared sad until

Kathy approached their table. Kathy loves all people, but she adores senior citizens and children. Kathy went and sat in a chair next to them. She said, "I have no idea what I want for dinner, so I looked across to see what you were having." Well, this looks pretty good; she proceeded to pick up a fork and take food from the lady's plate, and the lady started laughing. Next, she tried to take food from the gentleman's plate.

He told her that if she was going to take food off his plate, she had to give him a kiss. Sure enough, Kathy took the food and gave him a kiss on the cheek. I couldn't hear all that she said, but the people were laughing and enjoying themselves. I saw this elderly couple become twenty years younger in just a couple of minutes. They didn't even look like the same couple. Eventually, Kathy came back to our table. I looked back at the couple, and they were still laughing and pointing at Kathy. Kathy had just given them the gift of a special memory. They would probably leave there tonight and tell some friends or family members about the crazy woman who ate their food. Kathy gave them a priceless gift, and it cost her nothing.

As we were eating, the gentleman came up to her and kissed her on the cheek as he and his wife softly said, "Thank you." He then turned to me and said, "You have a special little lady here; take care of her." When they left, Kathy went back to eating as if nothing had happened and said, "Weren't they cute." I sat there, stared at her, and said, "Why did you do that?" She innocently said, "What do you mean?" Why did you go over to that couple and take the chance that you might be embarrassed? Those people could have taken offense to you touching their food. She looked at me and said, "I'm not so arrogant as to think that God put me here just for me."

There Are No Coincidences

A coincidence is nothing more than a miracle that God didn't get credit for. I always took all the miracles in my life for granted; things seemed to happen at just the right time. I can look back now and see how God worked in my life to bring me to where I am now. Today, I look for the miracles and make sure God gets all the credit He deserves.

"He performs wonders that cannot be fathomed, miracles that cannot be counted."

— Job 5:9

How many times in your own life has something happened unexpectedly, something that needed to happen just when it did? If you want to see more miracles, you need to get to know the miracle maker.

Get Involved with People

In the food service business, I was always around people but never involved with them. At the end of my day, I went home, had dinner, and turned on the television. No matter how many people I was with, whether family, friends, or work associates, I felt alone. I was never involved. God created us all to be part of one body, giving us certain gifts to build up others.

"Just as each of us has one body with many members, and these members do not all have the same function, so in Christ we who are many form one body, and each member belongs to all the others."

— Romans 12:4-5

At my church, I started to get involved in things that were happening. I helped with the Easter Sunrise Service, and in The Garden of Eatin' food service, I became a host and greeter and partnered in the Thanksgiving dinner for the homeless. I also helped with Autumnfest, an alternative to Halloween for children. I took classes at the church, baptized others at the beach baptism, organized a dinner for the pastors and staff, and played Santa Claus for the childcare ministry. I was a leader and a coach for small groups and got involved in anything else I could find. All those hours I used to throw away watching television became precious moments that I'll never forget.

Give to Others

For most of my life, I rarely gave to any charity, and when I did, it was very little. It would be unusual for me to give a hundred dollars or more in a year to any cause. My philosophy was what's mine is mine, and what I didn't have, I borrowed. I went bankrupt twice and was deeply in debt most of my life. I began giving one-tenth of everything I made to God. I also gave free offerings, donated to other charities, and gave anonymously to people in need. I spent a couple of hundred dollars on toys each year for underprivileged kids during Christmas. That year, I gave over twelve thousand dollars, and I was making over twenty thousand dollars a year less than I made in Ohio, and our house payment was over three times as much. The next year, the only debt I had was our home, car, and one credit card with a one-thousand-dollar balance. The only answer I could come up with was the one I found in:

"Give, and it will be given to you. A good measure, pressed down, shaken together, and running over, will be poured into your lap. For with the measure you use, it will be measured to you."

— **Luke 6:38**

God didn't only bless me with finances, but He blessed me with contentment. I was pleased with the man I was becoming, and I no longer needed all the stuff I used to buy.

Trust the One Who's Truly Trustworthy

Trusting people who were less than trustworthy burned me several times in my life, and I'm sure you have had the same experience. In the beginning, it was even difficult to trust God. I discovered that without complete trust, I couldn't move forward in my relationship with God. God has never let me down; He is always there when I need him, and I need him constantly.

"Commit your way to the LORD, Trust also in Him, And He shall bring it to pass. He shall bring forth your righteousness as the light, And your justice as the noonday."

— **Psalms 37:5-6**

Live in the Present

Yesterday is history, tomorrow a mystery, and today a gift; that's why it is called the present. This simple saying changed my life. I normally didn't receive my present because I was too busy living in the past.

I could waste hour after hour just contemplating different ways of living my life.

If I wasn't thinking about the past, I was worrying about the future. Worry. There is a worthless and harmful emotion. Worry is not planning. The definition of worry is mental distress or agitation. Yet as harmful as this emotion is, I spent a lot of my presents doing it. Every minute you think about the past or worry about the future is a present you didn't receive.

At Christmas, how many of your presents never got opened? Think, over just the last week, how many presents you didn't receive because you were living yesterday's situation or worrying about tomorrow? Everything that isn't in the present isn't real; it's only a thought. The only thing you can experience is right at this moment.

One thing about the present is that once it turns into the past, it's over; there is nothing you can do to change what just happened. Wouldn't it be great if we were computers, and when we did something wrong, we could just go to file, edit, and delete?

The only thing the past is good for is to learn. The past is a lesson, even though some of us try to make it a college education. The past should be a guidepost, not a hitching post.

It's not easy receiving your present. I challenged myself, in the course of a day, how often could I stay in the present? No matter how great it is to enjoy my present, I constantly catch myself slipping back into the past. I would be driving and trying to stay in the present, noticing the beautiful mountains, the blue skies, the ocean, and that great dark green Mercedes Benz. Boy, wouldn't it be great to afford a Mercedes Benz? After daydreaming for a minute or two, I would snap back into the present.

I was playing with a friend's 4-year-old daughter. Have you ever noticed a child playing? They have no inhibitions; they're not worried about what happened or what might happen tomorrow; they are just enjoying that moment. Have you ever heard a small child ask what time it is I have somewhere I need to be or something that must be done? For that moment, I was part of her life; I didn't think about anything else except just being with her and enjoying the moment together. I didn't worry about how silly I looked as I was on all fours making a variety of animal noises. I didn't think about work, what was for dinner, or the things that needed to be done later. Have you ever done that, where you worry about something you need to do so much it felt as if you did it several times instead of once? I did that all the time, but not that day.

Remember when your parents told you or you told your children to share their toys with others. That is what I started to do with my present, sharing it with others to get the full joy from it. I always thought I spent time with my wife, but the more I thought about it, the more time I spent watching television, reading, eating, or half-listening when she said something. I started really listening and asking questions to learn more about my wife and discovered all over again why I fell in love with her.

I enjoy watching a movie. I believe it's because this is something that totally engulfed me, and I didn't think about anything else. I went into this dark place and watched this movie, unaware of the people surrounding me or what was going on outside of the theatre. I would really get into the movie. I got so involved it was like being there. I would catch myself warning somebody that the killer was right there, and they were going to get her. Don't look at me; you've all done it.

We all have our own movies — the movies we create in our heads. Even though for a lot of us, we keep playing the same movies over and over again. I had great movies such as *I Can't Believe I Said That, Where Am I Going To Get The Money For That; I Wish I Hadn't Done That, I Didn't Mean It, If I Had It To Do Over Again, I'll Never Be Able To Do It, How Am I Going To Get Through Tomorrow* and many other features.

Even a great movie we can see a few times, but eventually, we get tired of watching it. However, the movies we create we see over and over and over again because, in our movies, the scenes have a way of changing. You don't quite remember the same things in exactly the same way; even the characters change from time to time. Sometimes, the villain becomes the hero, and vice versa. Every time I ran my movie, it was like living it over again. Sometimes, it got to the point where I didn't know what was the movie and what was real. I continued to torture myself time and time again, and as I tortured myself, I lost more and more of my presents.

I finally got tired of watching my old movies; I went outside, got involved with others, and breathed the air. I enjoyed my surroundings. I watched children play, started talking to people, and enjoyed the time I spent with my wife.

I learned my present only lasts a moment. I learned not to worry about what I didn't have and start enjoying what I did have. I also learned that if I enjoy all of my presents to the fullest, my future will take care of itself.

I leave you with this last thought. If you went to the doctor's and he said you only have a week to live, what would be the best way to live it? Worrying about what you should have done, worrying each day about the last, or enjoying every moment you are still alive? The present is a gift you only get once. Enjoy it.

Have an Attitude of Gratitude

Covet

"You shall not covet your neighbor's house; you shall not covet your neighbor's wife, nor his male servant, nor his female servant, nor his ox, nor his donkey, nor anything that is your neighbor's."

— **Exodus 20:17**

Have you ever wondered why covet would make God's top ten? It doesn't hurt anyone else; most people that you might covet something they possess wouldn't even know that you do. It appears to be more like wishing you had something your neighbor has and what could be wrong with that. The reason, I believe, is because it's showing discontentment and lack of gratitude. You're telling God you haven't given me enough, and I want more. If you covet other's belongings, you will never be grateful for the things God has already blessed you with, causing discontentment.

We always have a choice on how we are feeling by what we focus on. If you focus on the negative circumstances in your life or what you don't have, that causes depression, but God used thanksgiving in my life to begin the process of healing. When I was truly thankful for what I had, I wasn't focused on the things I thought I should have. My emotions went from anger and rejection to happiness and joy. I make it a habit when I see something that someone else has that I might be a little envious of. I stop and think of all the many blessings God has given me. If you're focusing on all the blessings God has given you, you won't have time to see anything else.

"Do not be anxious about anything, but in everything, by prayer and petition, with thanksgiving, present your requests to God."

Getting Over Depression

— **Philippians 4:6**

One of the cures for depression is to have an attitude of gratitude. Be thankful for what you have, and don't worry about what you don't have. The first book someone gave me when I got out of the hospital from my last, and I do mean last, suicide attempt was *Prison to Praise*. The book was about thanking God each day for everything you have in your life. You soon begin to realize all the good things God has blessed you with. We indeed learn from our mistakes, and once we realize that those, too, are blessings, we can see them in a different light. In a story about a Nazi concentration camp, one of the women would thank God each day for everything that she had.

One day, all the women in the quarters contracted lice, and Corrie Ten Boom thanked God for the lice. One of the other women yelled and asked her if she was crazy. How can you thank God for lice? A few days later, troops of German soldiers went into the camp, raping and killing women, but they didn't go into the quarters of those women because it was known that they all were infected with lice. If someone had told me at the time of my depression to be thankful for my life, I would have called them crazy, too. But God has bigger plans when we trust and praise Him!

I remember a time when I was walking around depressed and not knowing what to do. I sat on a bench and looked across the street. On the corner was a homeless man with a shopping cart, just sitting on the sidewalk. As I looked, I noticed he was looking at me; I thought what a terrible life that must be, not having any place to live or anyone to share your life with, not knowing when you're going to eat, and owning hardly anything. Then, I noticed him staring at me, and I wondered what he was thinking. He probably was thinking, what a terrible life that must be, having a nice place to live, being able to buy food whenever you want, having someone to love you, having the potential to do anything you want, and not appreciating any of it. I wonder which one of us was worse off?

Thanking God was one of the main turning points in my life. I started telling God what I was thankful for, and that minute began turning into a couple of minutes. Each time I prayed, it would get longer and longer because I became more aware of what God was doing in my life. Another person gave me a book by Stephen Covey entitled The 7 Habits of Highly Effective People, and another gave me motivational tapes from Anthony Robbins and Zig Ziglar. You might think that isn't very spiritual, but all of them had the same messages: Be grateful for what you already have, be a giver, treat others well, put your family first and they all referenced the importance of God and having faith.

During depression, it's hard to think of things we are grateful for because we are so focused on the bad things happening in our lives. One of the most important things to do when depressed is to thank God for His blessings in our lives. Here are a few examples:

1. My pulse — being alive!

"Your eyes saw my unformed body. All the days ordained for me were written in your book before one of them came to be."

— Psalms 139:16

2. Daily provisions

"Therefore, I tell you, do not worry about your life, what you will eat or drink, or about your body, what you will wear. Is not life more important than food, and the body more important than clothes? Look at the birds of the air; they do not sow or reap or store away in barns, and yet your heavenly Father feeds them. Are you not much more valuable than they? Who of you, by worrying, can add a single hour to his life?"

— Matthew 6:25

3. His protection

"But whoever listens to me will live in safety and be at ease, without fear of harm."

— **Proverbs 1:33**

4. Personal possessions

"I was young, and now I am old, yet I have never seen the righteous forsaken or their children begging for bread."

— **Psalm 37:25**

5. People that have made and are making a difference in my life

"As iron sharpens iron, so one man sharpens another."

— **Proverbs 27:17**

6. The problems I'm having

"Not only so, but we also rejoice in our sufferings because we know that suffering produces perseverance; perseverance, character; and character, hope. And hope does not disappoint us because God has poured out his love into our hearts by the Holy Spirit, whom he has given us."

— **Romans 5:3-5**

7. Pleasures I am experiencing

"For the LORD God is a sun and shield; the LORD bestows favor and honor; no good thing does he withhold from those whose walk is blameless."

— **Psalm 84:11**

8. God's plan for my life

"I will instruct you and teach you in the way you should go; I will guide you with My eye."

— **Psalms 32:8**

9. God's peace in my life

"And the peace of God, which transcends all understanding, will guard your hearts and your minds in Christ Jesus."

— **Philippians 4:7**

10. The place prepared for me for all eternity

"Do not let your hearts be troubled. Trust in God; trust also in me. In my Father's house are many rooms; if it were not so, I would have told you. I am going there to prepare a place for you. And if I go and prepare a place for you, I will come back and take you to be with me so that you also may be where I am. You know the way to the place where I am going."

— **John 14:1-4**

Listen Before Speaking

For most of my life, I had to be the one to speak. I needed to be the center of attention. During conversations, I wouldn't listen; I waited to find the opportunity to put my two cents in. So many times, I said the wrong things, used harmful words, and made stupid comments I couldn't take back. The old saying, "Sticks and stones will break your bones, but words can never hurt me," simply is not true. I've been hurt many times by the words others have spoken to me, and in turn, I have hurt others with mine.

"The tongue that brings healing is a tree of life, but a deceitful tongue crushes the spirit."

— Proverbs 15:4

Start Each Day Out Right

I've read several self-help books, and each one tells you to start your day in a positive way. Some tell you to ask yourself positive questions, to say uplifting things to yourself, to shout as soon as you get out of bed that today is going to be a great day, and other similar incentives. I agree that the way we start our day is very important, and it sets the mood for the entire day. I found that starting each day with my Lord in prayer and reading the Bible was the key to my recovery. I needed to spend that time thanking Him, learning from Him, speaking to Him, and listening to Him to know what He wanted me to do. When you spend time with God like this, you begin to realize who you are speaking to and how mighty He really is. What if you were going out to play basketball with some of your friends, and you knew you had Michael Jordan on your team? Would you be concerned about losing?

"Then you will call upon me and come and pray to me, and I will listen to you. 13 You will seek me and find me when you seek me with all your heart."

— **Jeremiah 29:12-13**

Pride is Not an Asset

Ego, pride, self-gratification, and whatever else you would like to call it were some of my worst enemies. It's what stopped me from ending a fight, from learning, caring about other people, and forgiving. This is a world where everyone has something to prove, no matter who it might hurt, and I was one of those people. I was so hung up on myself that I had to prove to everyone that I was right. If someone was telling me about themselves, I wouldn't let him finish before I started telling him about how wonderful I was. I needed so badly to get other people's respect and approval that I ended up driving people away. If someone didn't agree with me, I would tell myself that they didn't know what they were talking about or it was simply someone I didn't want to be associated with. Have you ever done that? Your ego was so big that you had to prove yourself superior to someone else.

Looking back on my life, the people that I was drawn toward were the people who seemed happy and just listened contently; they would add to the conversation when it seemed appropriate and were never confrontational. They were the people who seemed to simply enjoy others. I, on the other hand, was so self-involved in what I was going to say I was never really aware of the person I was talking with and, in turn, never got to know them. Pride didn't just hurt me; it hurt the people around me because I needed to give of myself to make a true connection with someone else, and I wasn't willing to share. It was amazing that I could be so full of pride and then also so self-condemning. It doesn't seem rational, does it? Believe me, being depressed has nothing to do with being rational.

"A man's pride brings him low, but a man of lowly spirit gains honor."

— Proverbs 29:23

Pride forces you to try to live up to your own expectations, and when you don't meet them, you either lower others to elevate yourself or go into depression because you fall short. I used to look up to those who used to boast about being self-made men, but the Lord showed me that I'm so much more; I'm a God-made man.

"Therefore, as it is written: 'Let him who boasts boast in the Lord.'"

— 1 Corinthians 1:31

Humility and Weakness Are Virtues

This was an unusual lesson for me to learn because, in our society, the humble and weak are the ones everyone walks on. I never saw anyone brag about how weak they were until I read the Bible when Paul said in

"That is why, for Christ's sake, I delight in weaknesses, in insults, in hardships, in persecutions, in difficulties. For when I am weak, then I am strong."

— 2 Corinthians 12:10

"He guides the humble in what is right and teaches them his way."

149

I look back on my life, and it made sense to me. I was so full of myself I didn't want to hear or learn anything else. When I was able to admit I had a long way to go but didn't have the strength to go any further, that's when God carried me so I could finish my journey.

Never Compare Myself to Others

I used to compare myself to a person that I wanted to be like, then get depressed because I realized how far I was from becoming like that person. Other times, I compared myself to someone who didn't have the things I had and filled myself with pride at their expense. I was so busy analyzing others that I didn't notice the person God had made in me.

"For we are God's workmanship, created in Christ Jesus to do good works, which God prepared in advance for us to do."

— Ephesians 2:10

I love this scripture because it tells me God has made me, and he made me for a purpose. He already has my path planned for me.

Encouragement

Normally, when people are depressed, they search for acceptance and encouragement from other people. Yet even though we might search to receive these things, we don't often give it. Most of us might think that the people we know don't deserve it, but that doesn't matter because we do it for our Lord to glorify Him. If we do it just to get praise from others, there is a great chance we won't get it, and we won't receive the blessing God has in store for us for being obedient to Him.

"Therefore encourage one another and build each other up, just as, in fact, you are doing."

— 1 Thessalonians 5:11

Desire to Pass the Test

"Blessed is the man who perseveres under trial because when he has stood the test, he will receive the crown of life that God has promised to those who love him."

— James 1:12

Let's say you will live to be eighty years old. Do you realize that you can't even compare how short one second is to eighty years, as eighty years is to eternity? A survey was taken, and ninety-five percent of the people polled believe there is a heaven. I always believed there was a heaven but didn't live my life as if I were going there. Is there anything you wouldn't do for just one second to make the rest of your life perfect?

I Have a Purpose

The question that went through my thoughts so often was, "Why am I here? What purpose do I have?" When I couldn't come up with an answer, I went into my deepest depression and made several suicide attempts. If something doesn't have a purpose, we throw it away. So many times, I wanted to throw away what I believed to be useless.

"I cry out to God Most High, to God, who fulfills his purpose for me."

— Psalms 57:2

I was continually trying to find the purpose in my life as if it were this one great thing. Now, each day, I discover a new reason God has me here. It may be as simple as listening to someone and helping them through their day. Who knows, someone I touch might go on to do great things. I now rest comfortably in knowing that no matter what comes along, I'm living according to God's plan. I stand on God's promise each day.

Knowing God's Word and Promises

I was struggling with thoughts of my job, finances, and health. It was so hard getting up in the morning and going to work, even though the first thing I do is pray and read the Word. One day, the church forwarded me an email from a young man who was suffering from depression. I emailed him back with my phone number, and shortly after, he called me. Filled with the Holy Spirit, I was able to comfort him, reciting God's promises. I told him life is one day at a time, God loves and is watching over him, that what he was experiencing was an attack from the enemy, and that God must have a high purpose for him; otherwise, why would Satan be bothering him. I gave him the scriptures God gave me in my worst of trials.

I told him it is not our job to figure out the ins and outs of our lives but to put those in God's hands and listen for His response. I shared parts of my testimony and answered all his questions using God's word. It was a wonderful time, as I could feel the peace that came over him. My wife, who was in the other room listening, said, "Maybe you should listen to what God puts on your hearts for others." She was right; I know the answers, I know where my joy comes from and what I should be doing, but when I leave my house in the morning after reading His word, I leave it behind. I'm like a soldier who goes out to war and realizes he left his gun behind. All he can do is try to dodge the bullets and hide the best he can so he doesn't get shot. He can't attack; he's defenseless without his weapon. That's me. I leave my weapon behind, and I'm a walking target for the fiery darts the enemy continues to shoot at me, and he is a good shot.

I don't need the physical book; God has planted His word in my heart. I just need to reach in and use it. I must get up in the morning ready for battle and come up with a strategy to use the one offensive weapon God has given me: His word. I know the enemy's battle plan; he uses it each day, and I need to be prepared to strike back, as Jesus did. Remember the forty days in the desert when Satan saw that Jesus was weak.

"Now when the tempter came to Him, he said, 'If You are the Son of God, command that these stones become bread.' But He answered and said, 'It is written, 'Man shall not live by bread alone, but by every word that proceeds from the mouth of God.''
Then the devil took Him up into the holy city, set Him on the pinnacle of the temple, and said to Him, 'If You are the Son of

God, throw Yourself down. For it is written: 'He shall give His angels charge over you,' and, 'In their hands, they shall bear you up, Lest you dash your foot against a stone.' Jesus said to him, 'It is written again, 'You shall not tempt the LORD your God.'' Again, the devil took Him up on an exceedingly high mountain and showed Him all the kingdoms of the world and their glory. And he said to Him, 'All these things I will give You if You will fall down and worship me.' Then Jesus said to him, 'Away with you, Satan! For it is written, 'You shall worship the LORD your God, and Him only you shall serve.' Then the devil left Him, and behold, angels came and ministered to Him.''

— Matthew 4:3-11

Jesus was packing, and all the devil could do was run. We are in a battle for our lives, so we come up with a strategy to use God's word and attack each day, knowing that He is right there by our side.

Journaling

Another tool that helped me stay focused and hear God clearer was SOAP. SOAP is a journaling technique that I was taught. It stands for Scripture, Observation, Application, and Prayer. What I would do is read a chapter in the Bible and see what verse God puts on my heart. I would then write that verse under Scripture. I would then date, give the journal entry a title, and then number that entry as a heading. Next, I would look at the scripture again and write what it meant to me, and that would be my Observation. Then, I would write how I'm going to apply what I just learned and how I am going to change to grow closer to God, and that would be my application. Last but certainly not least, I would write down a Prayer to ask God to direct me in my new path. There was always something special for me when I put things down in writing. You'll be surprised how little you must concentrate; the words will come to you as if someone else was writing it for you. I put down an example out of my journal to help get you started. Do yourself a favor and make a commitment to do this for thirty days and see what God has to say to you.

Date 3/12/12

I Need to Follow Jesus.

Page 1036

Scripture: Luke 14:27 And anyone who does not carry his cross and follow me cannot be my disciple.

Observation: I'm not carrying my cross fully. I need to submit fully to my Lord, yet I don't put Him first in my life. I get so caught up in this world, and in myself, at times, I leave Jesus out and give Him only a fraction of what He deserves from me. I'm only here because God wants me here, and this life I'm using is His. Not mine.

Application: I need to live this life as His. It's not when I have time for my Lord, but that all the time I have is His already. I need to submit fully to Christ's authority and live a life of righteousness that will be pleasing to my Savior.

Prayer: Dear Lord, you have blessed me so much, and I know I don't deserve any of it. All I have is yours, including the precious time you allow me to have. Show me how to use everything for your glory.

No Other Person Has Control Over You

I was counseling a young lady suffering from depression, and her outlook was the same as almost everyone I have spoken to. She allows what people say and do to affect her emotions. I can't tell you how many times I've heard; this person makes me so angry, and that person makes me feel worthless; if only this person would treat me better, I would be okay, and the list goes on. In actuality, no one can make you feel or act in any way; it's our decision to handle the way people treat or speak to us. The only person we have control over is ourselves. Circumstances do not affect us; how we decide to handle them does. There is nowhere in the Bible where it says to trust others; it only calls us to love them.

"Dear friends, since God so loved us, we also ought to love one another. No one has ever seen God, but if we love one another, God lives in us, and his love is made complete in us."

— 1 John 4:11–12

One of the worst abuses I can think of is child molestation or abuse, and yet some of these children grow strong and help others while others live their lives in quiet isolation. What's the difference between these situations? It's who you are listening to; is it the voice and opinion of someone else, or are you going to go to the only opinion that matters? There is only one person that you should always be listening to and taking His advice to heart, and that is God. What does God think of you? He loves you more than anyone can possibly love you.

"In this is love, not that we loved God, but that He loved us and sent His Son to be the propitiation for our sins."

— 1 John 4:10

He is here to help us get through this life.

"Take My yoke upon you and learn from Me, for I am gentle and lowly in heart, and you will find rest for your souls. For My yoke is easy, and My burden is light."

— **Matthew 11:29-30**

He'll always be there for you.

"Let your conduct be without covetousness; be content with such things as you have. For He Himself has said, 'I will never leave you nor forsake you.' So we may boldly say: 'The LORD is my helper; I will not fear. What can man do to me?'"

— **Hebrews 13:5-6**

I've found most people don't set out to hurt us, but they are sinners, just like us, and they don't know what to do or say; that is why God calls us to simply love. The young lady I was counseling was getting some of her low opinions of herself from a close family member. We talked, and I gave her the same advice the Bible gives about love. She went home that night and gave a hug to the person that has been hurting her, and he asked her do you think that will make anything better? How about giving me some respect instead. She was devastated and left the house crying. When I talked to her, I explained you can't react to someone else's reaction. He may not have given you the response you were hoping for, but believe me, you honored God and pleased Him, and that is all we are called to do. I told her to live her life for an audience of One and explained to her this was not going to be easy, and she couldn't do it on her own; she needed Jesus in her life to guide her.

"I will instruct you and teach you in the way you should go; I will counsel you and watch over you."

— Psalms 32:8

We need to constantly inquire about what we are supposed to be doing to be on the right path and to follow God's plans for our lives. We need to be in prayer every day and in His word to know what we should be doing. One day, when we are home, the only thing that will matter is what we did with the life God gave us. There will be no more pain or sorrow when we reach Home, and everyone around us will be loving and focused on our God, and the only words we'll hear will be loving and encouraging. However, while we are here, for this short time, let's set the goal of hearing these words from our Lord: "Well done, good and faithful servant. Welcome."

Have an Attitude That Honors God

Our attitudes and the way we treat people, especially the people who care for us, affect them. When I would get angry and start to yell, it affected the people around me. My family and friends would view it as if I didn't like them or they did something wrong. Most of us don't want to hurt others but can't control our lashing out because of the pain we feel inside and the need to get it out of our system. I typically didn't think about others and was only concerned with taking care of my immediate need, which was to get rid of the pain I currently felt. When I did that, I felt the pain of remorse later and hoped others would forget what I said. Could they, though?

Attitude Truths

- My attitude at the beginning of a task is the greatest determining factor of its outcome.
- My attitude determines other's attitudes toward me.
- My attitude affects my perspective of difficulties.
- My attitude can turn a difficulty into an opportunity.
- My attitude is often the only difference between success and failure.
- My attitude can get me hired or fired.
- My attitude, not my achievements, will bring me the greatest satisfaction.

- My attitude changes when I want it to change.
- My attitude is contagious.

We Have the Power to Be Content

Webster's definition of the word content is: "An inner peace and satisfaction where one is not disturbed or disquieted in whatever state or circumstances they are in." Contentment is an inner trait that is learned.

One of the major causes of depression is discontentment. When you are feeling depressed, it's because you are not content with an area of your life, whether it is your job, finances, spouse, family situation, or any other situation you might not be happy in. We allow our circumstances to take control of our emotional state. Paul wrote:

"Not that I speak in regard to need, for I have learned in whatever state I am to be content: I know how to be abased, and I know how to abound. Everywhere and in all things, I have learned both to be full and to be hungry, both to abound and to suffer. I can do all things through Christ who strengthens me."

— Philippians 4:11-13

Paul learned how to be content, and it didn't matter what his circumstances were. He didn't allow the things of

162

this world to control him. Paul's focus was on Jesus and heaven. He didn't let things control him; instead, he controlled the situation. We stay in discontentment or depression because we allow it to fester and take control of us instead of taking control over it. Has anyone ever asked you how you were doing, and you said, "Well, under the circumstances, not too bad?" What are you doing under the circumstances? Rise above them? We need to learn how to be content in everything. So how do we do that? We focus and think of why we should be content in the state that we are in. First, we are children of God, and when this life is over, we will be in our eternal home when we learn to praise God even in the worst situation; like Paul, you honor God, stop and praise God for all the blessings He has given you, know whatever situation you are in it's temporary, but you have life eternal in Christ. This life is a job placement test at best; what we do here and now will determine what we will be doing forever. Learn what you need to do to be content in any state and do it because you can do all things through Christ who strengthens you.

Things You Should Do When You Feel Depression Coming On

- Recognize what is depressing you. Is it real, or are you worrying about something that may happen or maybe even something imagined?

"Why are you downcast, O my soul? Why so disturbed within me? Put your hope in God, for I will yet praise him, my Savior and my God."

— **Psalms 42:5-6**

- Spiritually reorder your thinking and identify distorted thinking. Remind yourself God is in control and you're not alone.

"And the LORD, He is the One who goes before you. He will be with you. He will not leave you nor forsake you; do not fear nor be dismayed."

— **Deuteronomy 31:8**

- Replace negative thinking with honest prayer. Talk to God and tell Him how you're feeling. Job, Moses, Elijah, and Jonah all talked to God, wanting in despair, pouring out their feelings.

"Therefore, I will not keep silent; I will speak out in the anguish of my spirit; I will complain in the bitterness of my soul."

— Job 7:11

- Do not alienate yourself from others; share your feelings and ask for help.

"Therefore, as God's chosen people, holy and dearly loved, clothe yourselves with compassion, kindness, humility, gentleness, and patience. Bear with each other and forgive whatever grievances you may have against one another. Forgive as the Lord forgave you."

— Colossians 3:12-13

- Keep your focus on God and allow Him to fulfill His plan for your life.

"If then you were raised with Christ, seek those things which are above, where Christ is, sitting at the right hand of God. Set your mind on things above, not on things on the earth."

— Colossians 3:1-2

- Give your burdens to God; let Him fight your battles.

"Cast all your anxiety on him because he cares for you."

— 1 Peter 5:7

- I know it's hard to give up control of anything, let alone your whole life, but never cease to believe that none of us can even begin to imagine greater plans than the plans God has for our lives.

"However, as it is written: 'No eye has seen, no ear has heard, no mind has conceived what God has prepared for those who love him."

— **1 Corinthians 2:9**

Ask Better Questions of Yourself

How we feel is determined by the questions that we ask ourselves each day. If you ask questions like: Why does this always happen to me? Why don't people like me, why can't I do this? Why am I so stupid? Your brain will find answers even if it must make them up using past references, and the answers will not make you feel good. In the same way, if you ask yourself these questions, you will receive the answers. For example:

- How did I get so blessed to have the life I have?
- What can I do today to add to my joy?
- What am I happy about in my life right now?
- What can I do today to make God proud of me?
- How can I help someone else today?

You will get the answers because inside your spirit lies the answers. If you ask yourself questions leaning on God for the answer, He will always lead you to the right answer. The question that has made me aware of what is happening around me and has enriched my life is, "What does God want me to learn and do right here and now?" Every place I go, and in every situation, I ask myself this question, and the answers are remarkable. I'll ask myself that question when I talk or meet someone. "What does God want me to learn from this person?" I find myself listening intently to what that person has to say instead of having my mind wander. As a result, I've learned so much from others. Make up three questions you can ask yourself that would get you in a good state of mind:

Create Good Memories

I talk to people all the time about depression, and it's always the same: people are focused on things that have happened in the past or that may happen in the future, and they play that thought repeatedly in their minds. Every time they think of that, they experience all those frightening feelings all over again. God showed me what to do to get rid of those terrible thoughts, and that was to replace them with wonderful moments. You know those moments that bring joy to your heart and a smile to your face. God has produced some wonderful moments in my life, and all I had to do was show up. There have been so many wonderful moments I've lost count, and all I know is that they outweigh those bad moments. Paul nailed it when he said:

"Finally, brethren, whatever things are true, whatever things are noble, whatever things are just, whatever things are pure, whatever things are lovely, whatever things are of good report, if there is any virtue and if there is anything praiseworthy —
meditate on these things."

— Philippians 4:8

I used to be able to destroy my whole day by messing up one thing in the morning. I would stew about it all day long. Is there anyone that can relate? Now, no matter what I may say or do or how bad I mess up, I realize it's done and in the past. Instead of tearing myself down by saying how stupid I was, I would take it to God in prayer. One day, I was going to a meeting, and halfway there, I forgot my cell phone, and I knew I needed it.

Normally, I would have gone crazy and turned around, swearing at myself and sometimes hitting myself because I did such a stupid thing. I gave it to God, turned around, and thought to myself I need the phone, and if I'm late, I'm late. I got to the meeting a little late and found out the meeting was delayed. I still had to wait about fifteen minutes, and where I would have been upset about that in the past, I took the time to thank God that He took care of me and kept me safe. How would you like to have that feeling? How would you like to have the feeling that when you're driving, and someone cuts you off, instead of getting mad and upset, you take a moment to thank God you didn't get into an accident?

I start each day thanking God for all He has given me and all the ways He has blessed my life, and the list continues to grow. How do you avoid depression's fiery darts? Take up your shield of faith, knowing God is by your side.

Repent!

I believe the Bible breaks down the cause and cure for depression in just one word: Repent. I know nobody likes that word because what typically comes to mind is maybe John the Baptist yelling at the Pharisees to repent of their evil ways, or in any end-time movie, there is what looks like a homeless prophet commanding everyone to repent before it's too late. People who suffer from depression especially don't want to hear that they need to repent because it reminds them of one more thing that they are doing wrong to add to their list of many. God wants us to repent so we will draw closer to Him and be able to have joy in this life.

Picture yourself standing, and there to your right is your depression. You turn and face it, and there it is hopelessness, loneliness, anger, sexual abuse, betrayal, lost love, poor health, financial problems, paranoia, enduring sadness, self-loathing attitude, laziness, tiredness, irritability, anxiety, suicidal tendencies. You know these feelings oh too well; you see your depression all the time. We try to drown out our depression with drugs, alcohol, and lewd behavior and try to fill ourselves with the things of this world, hoping there might not be any room left for our depression. It's as if you can hear and see this monster that is destroying your life. You cover your ears and yell as loud as you can to drown it out and close your eyes tight so you can no longer see it, but it's only a matter of time before you lose your voice, your arms get tired, and you finally have to open your eyes. I want you to imagine you are staring at all the things that cause your depression and really look. See just beyond the torturous screams. Do you see him? Maybe only the top of his head or a horn or two, but he's there, and if you listen above the noise of the things that are hurting you so badly, you'll hear a hideous laugh. You know who that is, right?

The Slanderer (Revelations 12:10), The Tempter (Matthew 4:3), Ruler of Demons (Matthew 9:34), Evil One (Matthew 13:19), The Enemy of Humanity (Matthew 13:39), Father of Lies (John 8:44), Murderer (John 8:44), Our Adversary and a Roaring Lion to destroy us (1 Peter 5:8), Deceiver (Revelations 12:9), The Accuser (Revelations 12:10) and of course Satan or Devil. Depression is Satan's strongest weapon; he can incapacitate, torture, wound, and destroy his enemy, or he can use his RPG of depression suicide to annihilate us completely. Suicide is not the desire to die but the lack of will to go on. So, if you're not a Christian, he can condemn you to hell by keeping your focus away from God, and if you are a Christian, he can make you useless by not fulfilling the purpose God has created you for and steal the joy that God has in store for you.

How do you stop facing this depression each day? Repent! Do you do a 180° turn around, and guess who's there? The One who will never leave us or forsake us (Hebrews 13:5), the One who sacrificially loves us (John 3:16), the Almighty (Revelations 1:8), the One that is all-sufficient (2 Corinthians 9:8), the One who has great love for us (Ephesians 2:4-7), our help in trouble (Psalm 46:1), our defense and refuge (Psalm 59:16), our peace (Romans 1:7), our rewarder (Hebrews 11:6), our strength (Psalm 19:14), our comforter (John 14:16), our advocate (1 John 2:1), the way, truth and life (John 14:6), Dad (Mark 14:36), yes it's God. Picture Jesus with this warm smile on his face and his arms extended to you. What do you do? You take a step closer. As you make that first step, He then takes a step closer to you. It's important to know we need to make the first step as scripture states. *James 4:8 Draw near to God, and He will draw near to you.* You know you need to be much closer; in fact, you know you need to feel His embrace to be comforted by Him. You realize you have lived your life so far away from Him that you've forgotten that He was even there, but now you are coming home like the prodigal son. As you continue to draw near:

"And he arose and came to his father. But when he was still a great way off, his father saw him and had compassion, and ran and fell on his neck and kissed him."

— Luke 15:20

He now runs toward you as you run into His arms. You don't want to leave, you can't leave, but you hear over your shoulder Satan distracting you in the hope that you will turn around. So, how do you avoid turning back?

An old Cherokee is teaching his grandson about life. *"A fight is going on inside me,"* he said to the boy. *"It is a terrible fight, and it is between two wolves. One is evil – he is anger, envy, sorrow, regret, greed, arrogance, self-pity, guilt, resentment, inferiority, lies, false pride, superiority, and ego."* He continued, *"The other is good – he is joy, peace, love, hope, serenity, humility, kindness, benevolence, empathy, generosity, truth, compassion, and faith. The same fight is going on inside you — and inside every other person, too."* The grandson thought about it for a minute and then asked his grandfather, *"Which wolf will win?"* The old Cherokee simply replied, *"The one you feed."*

Feed your faith, read the Word every day, set up a time and a place where you can meditate on His word, memorize scripture and use them in your battle, be part of a Bible-believing church, not just attend, but be part of the body of Christ, surround yourself with your Christian brothers and sisters in home fellowship, serve others, go beyond meeting only your needs, but the needs of others, journal, write letters to God and most importantly pray. I would like to tell you that Satan will stop harassing you, but that's not his nature.

"The thief does not come except to steal, and to kill, and to destroy."

— John 10:10

Fortunately, God's nature is unconditional love, protection, and a promise of a life that will be worth living, as the rest of the verse is:

"I have come that they may have life and that they may have it more abundantly."

Chapter Eleven — Prayer

God's Prescription for Depression

Someone asked me if God had just healed me of my depression. I told them He didn't heal me like He did the blind, leper, or lame, but gave me a prescription that I would have to take each day for the rest of my life. This is a different type of prescription than the doctors used to give me for my depression. This one you can take as many times as you need in a day, and you'll never overdose, and hopefully, it will become habit-forming. The prescription was prayer, and I don't think I could make it through a day without it, and I don't try. However, there is a co-pay for this prescription; your part is that you love and obey Him. I still have times when I hear Satan's cry, but before I turn around too far, I pray and ask God for guidance. I can see why God didn't just heal me completely from my depression; he wanted to meet with me each day to guide me to where He wants me to be, and if I stay on what He prescribed for me, I know I'll be fine. Our life was designed from the beginning to live it with Jesus and not on our own:

April 6th, 1998, was the date of my last suicide attempt and the first time that I prayed to God. As I stated earlier, I had two prayer requests that day; the first was that God would just let me go and not enter hell or heaven, just make it as if I was never here. The second was that this experience wouldn't be painful, and He answered them both, and the answer was no. This was the beginning of a prayer life that gave me peace and joy.

I remember the day I received Jesus into my life; I was sitting in church. The Holy Spirit touched my heart, and I prayed that Jesus would come into my life. I remember saying to my Lord that I was tired of trying to live this life for myself and wanted to live it for Him, and He took me up on my offer.

That week, I called the pastors at the church and told them I had just been saved and wanted to serve in some way. I was asked about my background, and I told them I'd been in the food service industry all my life, including food service design. The pastor told me that was unbelievable because they had a company designing a large food service for the school and church. They were about to ask the board for approval, but no one knew anything about food service, so they asked if I could look over the plans and make any suggestions. After looking through the plans, I made page after page of recommendations. The pastor asked if I could meet with the board of elders and go over my suggestions. I was excited to help. In the evening, I arrived to find out there were about twenty people there, so I was a little nervous. They opened the meeting with a prayer from one of the elders. The gentleman reminded me of Morgan Freeman and had the voice to go with it. The prayer was beautiful, and I think it included every scripture in the bible. The louder he spoke, the smaller I felt as if I didn't deserve to be in the same room. When he was finished, I think God and all the angels gave him a standing ovation. Then, the spotlight was on me, and I was in my arena. I went through my notes about the pitfalls of the plans, along with my ideas for improving the layout.

Everyone seemed impressed, but then came the test. I was asked to give the closing prayer. My first instinct was to simply say no, but how would that look. With heads bowed, I started. I sounded like Porky Pig on speed. It was terrible; I don't even remember what I said. When I was done, I looked up, and I could still see the frightening stare on everyone's face and thinking how the angels must be booing. They must have thought I was speaking in tongues. I couldn't get out of there quick enough. By the time I got to my car, I was crying out loud. I was so embarrassed, and worst of all, I must have let Jesus down. As I started home and apologized to God for that horrible prayer, I felt Him next to me laughing. I felt as if He said that is not what prayer is all about; it's about talking to your Father. I'm now one of His children, and I think of the time in prayer as spending quality time with Dad.

Over the years, my prayer life became stronger as I spent more and more time in the word and with my Lord. When you're depressed, you can feel the anxiety coming, and I learned as soon as I realized what was happening, I went into prayer. Not long prayers, just simple ones such as Lord, please take this anxiety from me, Lord, I give you this burden I can't handle it alone, Lord, I need your peace, Help me, Lord, and other heartfelt cries to my loving Father. His word says He will never leave us or forsake us, and He always keeps His promise. I memorized scripture and stood on God's promises. As time went by, I depended on my Dad more and more, which I believe honors Him since He desires a close relationship with his children. As I got involved in more opportunities to serve, I would be leading, which gave me more time to pray in public. I began sharing my testimony at different churches, taught classes on depression, and did a Heaven study. I didn't realize it at the time, but God was grooming me for another purpose.

When Covid hit in 2020, I was laid off, and one day, I prayed and asked God What He wanted me to do with this time He had given me. That night, in a dream, I saw a shirt that read on one side, "Do You Need Prayer?" and on the other side, "I'll Pray with You." The next morning, I woke up and told my wife of the dream I had, and she told me it sounded like it was from God. I thought that it would be strange to walk in front of a bunch of strangers with a shirt like that and put it off. For the following week, I continued to have the same dream each night until I finally gave in and had the shirts made. I then prayed and asked God where He wanted me to go, and I felt led to go to the beach about four miles from my home.

At the time, that was the only place I could walk freely because of the Covid restrictions. My first day was July 4th, 2020. I was so nervous that I felt sick and wasn't sure if I could do it, but as soon as I got out of the car, the Holy Spirit took over. It wasn't long until I had my first prayer request from a woman who was vacationing there. A year later, I discovered that prayer was answered. I've been doing my prayer walk for over three years now, and

I'm enjoying the best part of my life. I've prayed for over two thousand people, seen miracles and healings, made some wonderful friends, and have shared my depression testimony numerous times. God was using the worst part of my life when I suffered from depression to be the greatest gift that I can offer to someone in need.

"Come and hear, all you who fear God, And I will declare what He has done for my soul."

— **Psalms 66:16**

I've not only met people who are suffering from depression but also others who are trying to cope with a loved one's suicide. God is my day planner, and each day, I have a divine appointment set up by Him. I was walking one day, and a young woman came up to me and told me she had seen me before and really needed prayer. She told me her husband just passed away about six days earlier, and she was really struggling. One thing that is wonderful about what I'm doing is that God does all the work. On my own, I would never know what to say in such a situation, but the Holy Spirit already knew.

After the Holy Spirit comforted this wonderful lady, I felt led to share my depression testimony. Thinking that is what she will be suffering with it after the loss of her husband. As I told her of my suicide attempts, she looked at me and told me that is how her husband died; he took his own life. I was able to comfort her by explaining that it was not her fault and the thoughts I had when I suffered from depression. I told her that people who commit suicide aren't thinking about dying; they just can't imagine living anymore and that they keep these thoughts deep within them and don't share them. After talking for a while, she asked if she could hug me, and I held her as I would hold my daughter. Before leaving, she looked at me and thanked me, saying that our talk really helped her. I walked away, thanking God for that special moment.

Another day on my walk, I heard someone yelling, "Would you really pray for me?" As I looked up, I saw a young man running from his apartment in a frantic state. I told him I would love to pray for him. Before I said a word, he started by just humbling himself and begging for forgiveness from God. One thing that I've learned is that I'm not out here thinking of how to pray but to simply be a vessel that the Holy Spirit can speak through. I'm like a Bluetooth speaker; I don't make the music — the music just comes out of me. The prayer was from a loving Father telling his son how much he is loved, the plans that he has for him, that he has everything he needs to fulfill the purpose he was created for, and that his Father would never leave him or forsake him.

After praying for him, I felt led to share my testimony on depression, and he began to cry. He looked into my eyes to tell me that he attempted suicide the night before and woke up and couldn't comprehend why he was still alive. He was confused and asked God why he was still alive and if he was supposed to be here to give him a sign. When he got himself together, he went for a walk, and as he was going down the driveway, there I was. I held him as we both cried and thanked God. I gave him my card with my phone number and website as I left. The next day, as I was walking, I heard someone yell my name. As I turned around, I saw him on an electric scooter yelling, "Isn't it a great day to be alive?" I stopped, cried, and thanked God for using this old sinner. I tell those that God has miraculously put in my path that God loves them so much that He sent this old fool to let you know He knows where they are and what they are going through, that He loves them and is always there whenever they need Him.

On another day, a man ran past me and asked if I would pray for him. He seemed so desperate, and I asked what he wanted prayer for, and he shared that he was in the middle of a divorce and had stage four cancer. He told me he felt that the cancer was caused because of sin in his life, and I told him if that was the case, we all would have stage four cancer. I asked if he believed in Jesus, and he shared that he used to walk with him, but it's been a long time, and he wasn't sure if he still was saved. He shared he has been contemplating suicide and that he felt he didn't want to live any longer. I told him if God thought you should be dead, we wouldn't be talking. I shared my testimony of depression, my past suicide attempts, and how God guided me through Satan's minefield. I told him the part where I told God I was His one mistake, and He has shown me over and over again He doesn't make mistakes. We went into prayer, and I stepped aside to allow the Holy Spirit to speak to him. The Holy Spirit told him that he would meet people in the same situation that he is in and that God would give him the courage and wisdom to be able to witness these people. For we are here to bring as many as we can into the kingdom of heaven, and there is no greater joy than that. After this amazing prayer, he broke down, and I hugged him, reassuring him that God loved him. Then, he recommitted his life to Jesus.

I keep a journal of my walks and post them to my website, gettingoverdepression.org. Each day, I meet someone new; I've seen answered prayer miracles and have developed wonderful friendships on my walks. I'm enjoying the best part of my life since I spend the day with the person I love the most, and at times, as I'm walking, I think I shouldn't be here. I should have been dead a long time ago, but it's just a reminder that God doesn't make mistakes.

This post is from the journal I keep on my prayer walk:

When the Fog Clears

Today when I left my house the sky was clear and sunny. It stayed that way until just before I parked my car, and the fog was so thick you could only see a few feet in front of you. I made it to the harbor, where I met a sister in Christ whom I'd spoken to before. She asked for prayer for her son, who had gone astray from his faith. After we prayed, I said I couldn't believe how thick this fog was; you could barely see the boats. She looked at me and said it wouldn't be long until the fog lifted and the beauty was revealed again. When I went on my way, I kept hearing what she said and thought most of my life; when I was suffering from depression, all I saw was the fog. I wasn't expecting to see anything beautiful, so I didn't and continued to stare into the fog. The fog is those moments that cripple our faith and limit our view. We can stay in the fog if we want, or we can be assured it will clear up to see the beauty it was covering up.

I recommend you take time in prayer to ask our Father What He wants you to do with this precious time He has given you. You have all the gifts and talents you need and a passion that he wants to use to help others. My prayer is God will give you the same overflowing joy He has blessed me with.

Chapter Twelve — We Need to Be Homesick

My wife and I took a mission trip to an orphanage in Mexico. It was an awesome experience, and at the end of each day, our group would sit around a campfire for a devotional. One night, I was asked to lead the devotional, and God placed on my heart what He wanted me to discuss. I started by going around the group and asking each person, "When I say heaven, what comes to your mind?" I also gave them an opportunity to pass if they couldn't think of something right away. The first couple of people passed, then the next said Jesus, then another love, but no one gave an answer as if heaven was on their mind.

I explained we had only been there for a couple of days without taking a shower and sleeping in tents and that I was already homesick. I've been thinking of a nice hot shower, a comfortable bed, relaxing on the couch, going to the kitchen whenever I want to get something to eat, and other comforts I missed. Yet I live in a world where sin is accepted, hate outweighs love, sexual immorality is just an alternative lifestyle, pollution, corruption, sickness, and lust. This is truly Satan's playground. I know when my time is up on this earth, it will be time to go home, a beautiful place, too beautiful to be described, a place where I'm going to live with the one person who loves me more than anyone could for all eternity. Yet, it hardly crosses my mind. How can I get so homesick for a temporary home on this earth and not homesick for my eternal home?

A couple of days after we returned from Mexico, I was talking with someone and told them about my devotion to heaven. She asked if I had ever read a book by Randy Alcorn called, "Heaven." I told her I never heard of it, and she loaned me her copy. It was the most amazing and wonderful book, except for the Bible, that I had ever read. Using scripture, the book explains what heaven will be like, and it was so reassuring and exciting I couldn't put it down.

When we are depressed, we give up hope and even the possibility of becoming happy because we are unable to imagine that. It is also why we don't think of heaven because we don't know what it's going to be like. Some of us have images of doing nothing for all eternity in a constant state of peaceful bliss. How boring is that? Some think we will be just spirit beings like the angels, others picture themselves just sitting around worshipping God, and others may think we will have a mindless existence and will have no desire to do anything except what we will be programmed to do. No wonder we don't look forward to going home. Randy Alcorn's book, however, paints a totally different place, a place where you can't wait to come home.

"But in keeping with his promise, we are looking forward to a new heaven and a new earth, the home of righteousness."

— **2 Peter 3:13**

Again, using scripture, the book explains if we were to pass away now, we would be with Jesus in paradise, like the thief who was crucified next to Jesus.

"Jesus answered him, 'I tell you the truth, today you will be with me in paradise.'"

— **Luke 23:43**

This will be a wonderful place, but not our eternal home.

Mr. Alcorn explains that our family and friends who have gone ahead will be able to see us, we will recognize people when we get there, and we will have a purpose that involves the gifts and abilities God has given us on earth.

"Then I saw a new heaven and a new earth, for the first heaven and the first earth had passed away, and there was no longer any sea. I saw the Holy City, the new Jerusalem, coming down

out of heaven from God, prepared as a bride beautifully dressed
for her husband. And I heard a loud voice from the throne
saying, 'Now the dwelling of God is with men, and he will live
with them. They will be his people, and God himself will be with
them and be their God. He will wipe every tear from their eyes.
There will be no more death or mourning or crying or pain, for
the old order of things has passed away.' He who was seated on
the throne said, 'I am making everything new!' Then he said,
'Write this down, for these words are trustworthy and true.'"

— **Revelations 21:1-5**

The exciting part for me was when Jesus returned and set up His Kingdom, He was going to make a new heaven and earth. Imagine a new heaven and earth without any sin, brand new with no destruction, and we each get to start at the beginning in the presence of God. We will have a new and perfect body.

"But our citizenship is in heaven. And we eagerly await a Savior
from there, the Lord Jesus Christ, who, by the power that
enables him to bring everything under his control, will
transform our lowly bodies so that they will be like his glorious
body."

— **Philippians 3:20-21**

We Need to Be Homesick

We will recognize our loved ones, we will get to meet people we only read about in history books and the Bible, we will remember what we did on earth, and we will have a job to do, the job we were created to do from the beginning. The book goes into detail of what we might expect in our new home.

"In my Father's house are many rooms; if it were not so, I would have told you. I am going there to prepare a place for you."

— **John 14:2**

Other questions the book answers are: will we rule with Christ? Will there be space and time? Will we have the sun, moon, oceans, and weather? Will we be ourselves? What will our bodies be like? Will we eat and drink, what will our daily lives be like, who will we meet, will there be animals? Will we see our pets again? And so many more questions will be answered. In the book, Heaven is a section entitled A Word to the Depressed, and it reads as follows:

The fact that heaven will be wonderful shouldn't tempt us to take shortcuts to get there. If you're depressed, you may imagine your life has no purpose; you couldn't be more wrong. As long as God keeps you here on Earth, it's exactly where He wants you. He's preparing you for another world. He knows precisely what He's doing. Through your suffering, difficulty, and depression, he's expanding your capacity for eternal joy. Our lives on earth are a training camp to ready us for Heaven.

I know depression can be debilitating. Many godly people have experienced it. But if you are considering taking your own life, recognize this as the devil's temptation. Jesus said that Satan is a liar and a murderer (John 8:44). He tells lies because he wants to destroy you (1 Peter 5:8). Don't listen to the liar. Listen to Jesus, the truth-teller (John 8:32; 14:6). Don't make a terrible ending to your life's story-finish your God-given course on Earth. When He's done, before-he'll take you home in his own time and way. Meanwhile, God has a purpose for you here on this earth. Don't desert your post.

If you don't know Jesus, confess your sins and embrace his death and resurrection on your behalf. If you don't know him, make your daily decisions in light of your destiny. Ask yourself what you can do today, next week, next year, or decades from now to write the best ending to this volume of your life's story — a story that will continue gloriously in the new universe.

By God's grace, use the time you have left on the present Earth to store up for yourself treasures on the new earth, to be laid at Christ's feet for his glory (Revelations 4:10). Then look forward to meeting in Heaven Jesus himself. As well as those touched by your Christ-exalting choices.

"A little while and the wicked will be no more; though you look for them, they will not be found. But the meek will inherit the land and enjoy great peace."

— Psalms 37:10-11

So why are you still here? Because God is giving you a chance to store up treasures and earn rewards that will last for all eternity.

"Live such good lives among the pagans that, though they accuse you of doing wrong, they may see your good deeds and glorify God on the day he visits us."

— 1 Peter 2:12

"And that you, O Lord, are loving. Surely, you will reward each person according to what he has done."

— Psalms 62:12

"But I said, 'I have labored to no purpose; I have spent my strength in vain and for nothing. Yet what is due me is in the LORD's hand, and my reward is with my God.'"

— Isaiah 49:4

"Great are your purposes, and mighty are your deeds. Your eyes are open to all the ways of men; you reward everyone according to his conduct and as his deeds deserve."

— **Jeremiah 32:19**

"Rejoice and be glad, because great is your reward in heaven, for in the same way they persecuted the prophets who were before you."

— **Matthew 5:12**

"Since you know that you will receive an inheritance from the Lord as a reward. It is the Lord Christ you are serving."

— **Colossians 3:24**

"Behold, I am coming soon! My reward is with me, and I will give to everyone according to what he has done."

— **Revelations 22:12**

We will only be here on this earth for a little while longer before going home. I remember when my parents would go on vacation, and my sister and I stayed home with our grandparents. We couldn't wait until they came home because they would bring us back something from their journey. When you get home, what will you bring home from your journey to your Father? Will it be something priceless like a life lived for Him, doing His will? I so desperately want to hear my Lord say to me:

"His master replied, 'Well done, good and faithful servant! You have been faithful with a few things; I will put you in charge of many things. Come and share your master's happiness!'"

— **Matthew 25:21**

We will get to experience Eden like Adam and Eve, only this time without the sin. When you think about it, it makes sense that God doesn't make mistakes, and so many think that the Garden of Eden was a mistake, because of what Adam and Eve did, but how else could God find those who would truly love and trust Him. He chooses those who, through the trials and tribulations of this life and the sin of this world, still say I trust you, Father, and thank you for the sacrifice of your Son so that I may call this home with you.

God has shown me so much on my journey, but two things stand out. First, our life is only a day at a time, as stated in the Lord's prayer *Matthew 6:11: Give us this day our daily bread.* God gave the Israelites manna only one day at a time, and *Psalms 118:24 This is the day the LORD has made; We will rejoice and be glad in it.* So, live in the moment for that is all we have. The second thing is to worry only about what you can control, then realize the only thing you can control is yourself. So, instead of trying to change others or

194

situations, focus on yourself and be the best you can be for God. When you do that, you will begin your journey of drawing closer to Him and understand God's love for you and the purpose you were created for.

"For I know the thoughts that I think toward you, says the LORD, thoughts of peace and not of evil, to give you a future and a hope."

— **Jeremiah 29:11**

Made in the USA
Las Vegas, NV
08 February 2024